MY BODY
MY CHOICE

The Fight for
Abortion Rights

ROBIN STEVENSON

illustrations by
Meags Fitzgerald

ORCA BOOK PUBLISHERS

Library and Archives Canada Cataloguing in Publication

Stevenson, Robin, 1968–, author
My body, my choice: the fight for abortion rights / Robin Stevenson.

(Orca issues)
Includes bibliographical references and index.
Issued in print and electronic formats.
ISBN 978-1-4598-1712-8 (softcover).—ISBN 978-1-4598-1713-5 (PDF).—
ISBN 978-1-4598-1714-2 (EPUB)

1. Abortion—Juvenile literature. I. Title.
HQ767.S74 2019   j362.19'888   C2018-904778-x
                        C2018-904779-8

Library of Congress Control Number: 2018954165
Simultaneously published in Canada and the United States in 2019

Summary: This nonfiction book for teens examines the ongoing fight for abortion rights and reproductive justice.

Orca Book Publishers gratefully acknowledges the support for its publishing programs provided by the following agencies: the Government of Canada, the Canada Council for the Arts and the Province of British Columbia through the BC Arts Council and the Book Publishing Tax Credit.

Interior illustrations by Meags Fitzgerald

Edited by Sarah N. Harvey
Design by Teresa Bubela
Cover illustrations from photos by Jacob Lund/Shutterstock.com

ORCA BOOK PUBLISHERS
orcabook.com

Printed and bound in China.

22 21 20 19 • 4 3 2 1

*To my friend Pat Smith, with so much love and respect,
and to the many dedicated, compassionate and hardworking people
around the world who are fighting for reproductive rights
and reproductive justice for all.*

CONTENTS

CHAPTER FOUR: FIGHTING FOR
SAFE ABORTION AROUND THE WORLD / 83

CHAPTER FIVE: THE WAY FORWARD:
STORIES FROM THE FRONT LINES / 119

INTRODUCTION

You've probably seen news reports about people marching to protect abortion rights. Or perhaps you've seen anti-abortion protesters standing in front of a clinic. Maybe you have a friend or a family member who told you that they chose to end a pregnancy. Maybe you've had an abortion yourself.

Abortion is one of the most commonly performed medical procedures. In North America one in four women will have an abortion by the age of forty-five. So you almost certainly know someone who has had an abortion—even if you don't think you do. Because there is still **stigma** associated with abortion, many people don't talk about their experiences.

People who think abortion is wrong often try to have it made illegal or at least difficult to get. But this doesn't make abortion any less common—it just makes it dangerous. When done by a trained doctor, abortion is safe—ten times safer than childbirth. Before abortion was legalized, though, many women in Canada and the United States died or were terribly injured by unsafe illegal abortions. And around the world tens of thousands of women still die from unsafe abortions every year.

During the 1970 Women's Strike for Equality, tens of thousands of feminists marched through the streets of New York and gathered at many more organized demonstrations across the country—like this one in Washington, DC. One of their goals was free abortion on demand.

Over the last fifty years people who support abortion rights have been fighting hard to create a world in which access to safe and legal abortions is guaranteed. Opposition has been intense and sometimes violent. Victories have been hard won, and women's right to control their own bodies remains under threat. All around the world people are speaking out about abortion, breaking the silence and shattering **taboos**. They are working to educate others and **lobbying** their governments. They are raising money to help those who can't afford abortions, and they are harnessing the power of the Internet to help people get safe abortions in countries where abortion is a crime.

In this book you will meet all kinds of activists. The women who drove across Canada in the 1970 Abortion Caravan. The feminists in Chicago who taught themselves to do safe abortions during the illegal-abortion era. The women who use a boat to provide abortions in international waters. Community groups using **crowdfunding** to open abortion clinics, and students building websites to help people access abortion services. Doctors who put their lives on the line to provide abortions despite daily harassment and threats of violence.

The March for Choice in Dublin, Ireland, in 2012.

Young reproductive rights advocates all over the world who educate others, lobby for change and help people who are facing unwanted pregnancies.

The long fight for abortion rights is being picked up by a new generation of courageous, creative and passionate activists. This book is about the history—and the future—of that fight.

WHAT IS AN ABORTION?

A *spontaneous abortion*, or *miscarriage*, is when a pregnancy ends naturally before the fetus has developed enough to survive. This happens in about 10 to 25 percent of all pregnancies. When people speak about abortion, they generally mean **induced abortion**, which is when a pregnancy is ended deliberately. In this book, the word *abortion* refers to induced abortions. The vast majority—around 90 percent—of these abortions occur during the *first trimester* (first twelve weeks) of pregnancy.

There are two ways of ending a pregnancy: *surgical abortion* and *medical abortion*. In Canada and the United States, both procedures are common and safe.

SURGICAL ABORTION

The majority of abortions in North America are surgical abortions, provided in medical clinics or hospitals. The most common type of surgical abortion occurs in the first trimester of pregnancy and is known as suction abortion, or vacuum aspiration. In this procedure, the patient's *cervix* is dilated, and a thin straw called a cannula is inserted. The cannula is attached to a tube, and gentle suction is used to empty the contents of the uterus (or womb). The whole procedure takes less than five minutes.

Another procedure is called dilation and evacuation, or D and E. It's generally used for abortions a little later in pregnancy, and it uses both suction and medical instruments to empty the uterus. This takes a little longer—up to fifteen minutes.

During both types of procedure, most patients experience some cramping, similar to menstrual cramps and varying from mild to more severe. They receive pain medication and sometimes sedation to help them relax, and they can usually return to normal activities the next day.

MEDICAL ABORTION

In the United States, about 20 percent of abortions involve not surgery, but pills. In some countries, the majority of abortions are done this way. This type of abortion is called a medication, or medical, abortion. It uses a combination of prescription drugs to end the pregnancy. These drugs are **mifepristone** and **misoprostol**, but the pairing of them is often just referred to as "the abortion pill." The abortion pill is also known as **RU-486**, and in Canada it is sold as **Mifegymiso**. (Abortion pills are different from **emergency contraception**, also called the **morning-after pill**, or **plan B**, which prevents pregnancy.)

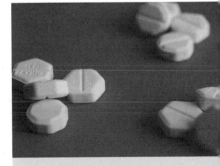

Abortion pills are a safe and effective way of ending a pregnancy.

In the first ten weeks of pregnancy, medical abortion offers an alternative to surgical abortion. The pills induce an abortion similar to a natural miscarriage, causing cramping and bleeding to empty the uterus—like a very heavy period that lasts from several hours to a couple of days. The abortion can happen at home, with

These reproductive rights advocates from the National Network of Abortion Funds have an important message: Because abortion is so common, we all know and care about people who have had abortions...whether we are aware of it or not.

over-the-counter pain medication to manage the discomfort of the cramping. Just as with a surgical abortion, most people are able to return to normal activities the next day. Studies show that medical abortion is a safe and effective alternative to surgical abortion.

WHO HAS ABORTIONS?

Many people have abortions: around the world there are well over 50 million abortions every year. In Canada about 40 percent of all pregnancies are unplanned. Roughly half of these pregnancies are carried to term, and the other half are terminated. In the United States about a million abortions are performed every year. There, around 12 percent of abortion patients are in their teens. In Canada about half are under age twenty-five. Many people who have abortions already have at least one child. Nearly half are living with a male partner, and more than half were using a method of **contraception** during the month they became pregnant.

People from all religious backgrounds get abortions. A 2014 US study found that 17 percent of abortion patients described themselves as Protestant, 13 percent as evangelical Protestant,

24 percent as Catholic, and 38 percent as having no religion. The remaining 8 percent described themselves as belonging to another religion.

And people from all cultural, racial and ethnic backgrounds have abortions. Immigrants to the United States have abortions at about the same rate as those born there. Some people who have abortions are high school, college or university students. Many people who have abortions are poor or low-income. And while most people who have abortions are women, some are not— **transgender** men and **non-binary** people who have uteruses can become pregnant and may experience unwanted pregnancies.

People of all religions, nationalities, income levels and racial and cultural backgrounds choose to end pregnancies and need access to abortion services.

People choose to have abortions for many different reasons. Some decide to have an abortion because they feel they cannot afford to raise a child or because they are caring for others. Others feel that having a child would interfere with their ability to work or go to school. Some people simply don't want children.

All these people—encompassing all ages, religions, nationalities, beliefs and life circumstances—have one thing in common. They are pregnant and they do not want to be.

A NOTE FROM THE AUTHOR:

Much of the historical material, research and statistics I have drawn on for this book refers specifically to women. In those cases, my language reflects the source material. In all other places, I have tried to use trans-inclusive language whenever referring to people who experience pregnancy or have abortions.

ADVICE TO MARRIED LADIES.—MAD-AME RESTELL, Professor of Midwifery, having over thirty years' successful practice in this city, guarantees a safe and immediate removal of all special irregularities and obstructions in females, with or without medicine, at one interview, or by mail. Can be consulted with the utmost confidence at No. 162 Chambers-st. Her infalli-ble French Female Pills, No. 1, price $1, or No. 2 which are four degrees stronger than No. 1, and can never fail, are safe and healthy, price $5, can be sent by mail. Also sold at the druggist's, No. 152 Greenwich-st, near Liber-y-st. Madame RESTELL deems it her duty to caution dies against imitators, who not only deprive them of r means, but their health.

CHAPTER ONE

LOOKING BACK: THE HISTORY OF ABORTION

Around the world, women have always used herbs and other preparations to end unwanted pregnancies. According to Chinese folklore, the mythical emperor Shennong used highly toxic mercury to induce abortion 5,000 years ago. The Egyptian *Ebers Papyrus*—one of the world's oldest preserved medical documents, written over 3,500 years ago—contains the earliest written evidence of abortion.

In ancient Greece, the philosopher Plato wrote that providing abortions was one of the important roles played by **midwives**. Five hundred years later, the Greek physician Soranus wrote a medical textbook that actually described ways of

The Ebers Papyrus is written on a papyrus scroll about 20 meters long and contains remedies for inducing abortion using ingredients such as acacia gum, dates and honey.

inducing abortion—none of which were effective, and some of which were actually dangerous. He advised that the pregnant woman should try "walking about energetically and being shaken by the means of draught animals; she should also leap energetically and carry things which are heavy beyond her strength."

He recommended various herbal recipes, both for drinking and for bathing in, and suggested that the woman "be bled, and a relatively great quantity taken away." This last recommendation sounds alarming but is hardly surprising: bloodletting was one of the most common treatments for a wide range of ailments from at least the fifth century BCE until the late nineteenth century.

In the Middle Ages, pregnancy was not considered to begin until the time of "quickening," when the woman first felt the movements of the fetus. This was usually around the sixteenth to eighteenth week of pregnancy. Until that happened she was not considered pregnant, and women often took herbal concoctions in hopes that they would bring on menstruation.

In many places, women's right to control their fertility and seek an early end to unwanted pregnancies was not restricted until fairly recently. So what changed?

RACISM AND POPULATION CONTROL

In colonial America, following the old English law, abortion was legal at least until quickening. At the time the United States Constitution was adopted in 1787, abortions were openly advertised and commonly performed. Contraception (birth control) was also used, although it was less effective than modern methods of preventing pregnancy. It wasn't until the mid-1800s that states began passing laws that made abortion illegal.

One major reason for the criminalization of birth control and abortion was rooted in racism. Lawmakers wanted to make certain that white people remained a large majority, which meant ensuring that white women had lots of babies. At the same time abortion was being criminalized, racist immigration policies began limiting who could enter the country. The government

In an herbal guide from the Middle Ages, women were pictured grinding pennyroyal with a mortar and pestle, a popular abortifacient method dating back to Hippocratic times. In the late 1800s, "pennyroyal pills" were sold by druggists along with other herbal remedies, such as " tansy, rue, roots and seeds of the cotton plant, cedar gum, and camphor", techniques originally brought from Africa to the United States.

PRESERVE

4000 YEARS FOR CHOICE!

feared that new immigrants, whose birth rates were higher than those of white women, would come to dominate the population.

The history of reproductive rights and freedom is intertwined with the history of racism. As far back as the 1600s, white European settlers actively used a number of "population control" strategies to increase their wealth and dominance. In 1662 the first law was passed that used reproduction for this purpose. This new law said that the legal status of a baby—whether the baby was a slave or free—would now be the same as the mother's. This meant that babies born to enslaved women were the property of the slaveholders. Many children born into slavery were sold away from their mothers. After Congress passed the Act Prohibiting Importation of Slaves in 1807, slaveholders wanted to make sure that enslaved women became pregnant and gave birth, as this would create future slaves. Rape and forced reproduction were extremely common.

Enslaved women found ways to stand together. They shared information about ways to avoid pregnancy using herbs as contraceptives. Some were midwives who helped women abort their pregnancies in secret. Refusing to bring a child into a life of slavery—and refusing to produce a new slave for the slaveholder—was one of the ways in which enslaved women resisted during the long years of slavery.

THE CRIMINALIZATION OF ABORTION

All surgical procedures, including abortion, were risky in the 1800s. Childbirth was also dangerous, and many mothers and infants died. As science developed and began to influence medical practice, childbirth and most surgeries became safer. But abortion remained risky, because with the new laws being

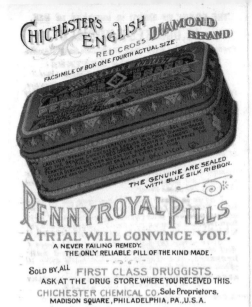

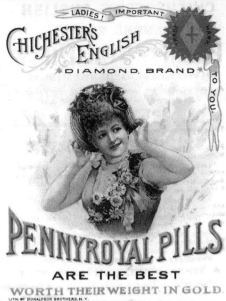

Advertisements for pills to bring on menstruation were common during the Victorian era and into the early 1900s. Many of these pills were ineffective, and some were highly toxic: the dose of pennyroyal needed to cause an abortion could be fatal or cause permanent liver and kidney damage to the person taking it.

passed, most women who needed abortions had no alternative but to get them illegally. Millions of women had illegal abortions or attempted to self-induce abortion, and thousands of them died. Despite the risks, women were desperate to control their own bodies and lives, and abortion was even more common in the late 1800s than it is today.

The male-dominated medical profession did not want competition from midwives and other, often female, practitioners. They argued that abortion was both morally wrong and dangerous, and they pushed for it to be criminalized. By 1910 nearly every state had passed laws making abortion a criminal offense except when it was necessary—in a doctor's judgment—to save the woman's life. This meant that no one other than a doctor could legally perform an abortion.

In Canada abortion was banned in 1869, with a penalty of life in prison for any woman who tried to end her pregnancy and for anyone who assisted her. In 1892 Parliament enacted

A CERTAIN REMEDY

One practitioner during the 1800s was Ann Trow Lohman, who for 40 years, under the name Madame Restell, openly advertised and provided abortion services in New York City. She had no medical training, but she sold folk remedies containing common ingredients believed to end pregnancy. They were advertised as pills to "regulate the monthly cycle." If those herbal remedies failed, Madame Restell offered surgical abortions. She was so well known that the word *Restellism* came to mean "abortion." At the time she began her work, abortion was not yet criminalized, but later, after new laws were passed, she was arrested and charged. In 1878 she died by suicide.

From top: Ann Lohman, better known as Madame Restell; the luxurious New York mansion where she lived with her husband, Charles R. Lohman; a classified ad from a New York newspaper, April 1840, in which Madame Restell promotes her "Preventive Powders for married ladies, whose health forbids a too rapid increase of family"; the New York Illustrated Times reports the arrest of Madame Restell.

the first Criminal Code, which not only prohibited abortion, but also forbade selling, distributing and advertising birth control. Social worker Dorothea Palmer was arrested and charged in 1936 with offering birth-control information. She stated, "I expected trouble sooner or later. I may get a few months in prison for it. In view of the desperate conditions I have seen in the homes I have visited, I would most certainly do the same thing again the moment I was liberated."

Dorothea Palmer's trial lasted six months before the judge ruled in her favor. The ruling was based not on concern for women's rights but on a desire to control population growth among the poor.

In both Canada and the United States, doctors who performed abortions for compassionate or medical reasons could be prosecuted. However, many family doctors performed abortions in the first half of the twentieth century despite the law. Experts estimate that more than a quarter of all pregnancies ended in abortion during the Great Depression of 1929–1939. In those days it was more common for family doctors to do surgery, and some saw helping women end unwanted pregnancies as merely one part of providing care. Women who had money and a private doctor could sometimes get safe abortions. Poor women, however, could not—and they suffered the most as a result.

After the Depression ended, white women were encouraged to have many children. Those who put their careers ahead of motherhood, chose not to have children or didn't have enough children were strongly disapproved of. So was abortion. For women of color, though, the messages were very different. After the abolition of slavery—when their babies no longer meant more wealth for slaveholders—public policies began discouraging Black women from having children. (See sidebar on page 29 for more about forced sterilization.) Ignoring the many factors that contributed to poverty—such as limited employment opportunities for people of color, poor schools and lack of medical care—policy makers suggested that women of color were being "irresponsible" by having children they could not afford. This type of thinking continued throughout the 1900s and is still echoed by some right-wing politicians today.

THE ILLEGAL-ABORTION ERA

The fact that it was illegal did not stop women from getting abortions. Women facing unwanted pregnancies have always found ways to end them, no matter how high the risk. It is impossible to know the exact numbers, but in the 1950s and 1960s hundreds of thousands of illegal abortions took place every year. Thousands of women died or suffered serious medical problems after having illegal "back alley" abortions performed by untrained people working in unsanitary conditions. Many thousands more died or were horribly injured as a result of attempting to end their pregnancies themselves. Hospital staff treated huge numbers of women for infection and injury following abortions provided without adequate skill and care.

Wealthier women could sometimes travel to countries like Sweden, where abortion was available, or find physicians closer to home who would do the procedure for a large fee. Poor women had fewer options. They were the most likely to suffer at the hands of incompetent abortion providers or to risk their lives by trying to end their pregnancies themselves. Illegal abortion accounted for 17 percent of maternal deaths—and many more women were left with injuries that caused illness, pain and infertility.

For unmarried women in the 1950s and '60s, an unwanted pregnancy was a terrifying prospect. Being single and pregnant was considered scandalous—a woman was socially stigmatized for having a child without a husband. But pregnancy was also difficult to avoid: in many parts of Canada and the United States, unmarried women were not allowed to get birth control, and many others simply could not afford it.

AN AWFUL SITUATION

As a young graduate from the University of British Columbia's medical school, Garson Romalis chose to do his residency and internship at Cook County Hospital, in the heart of Chicago, Illinois, in the early 1960s. An entire ward was filled with women recovering from botched abortions. "About 90 percent of the patients were there with complications of septic abortion," Dr. Romalis said in a 2008 speech at the University of Toronto law school. "The ward had about 40 beds, in addition to extra beds which lined the halls. Each day we admitted between 10 to 30 septic abortion patients. We had about one death a month, usually from septic shock associated with hemorrhage...I will never forget the jaundiced woman in liver and kidney failure, in septic shock, with very severe anemia, whose life we were unable to save."

His experience was not unusual. Across the country there were hundreds of septic abortion wards, all filled with women recovering—or sometimes dying—after attempting to end their pregnancies. Dr. Daniel Mishell was an obstetrician-gynecologist (OBGYN) who worked in California hospitals during the same time period. "We had ladies who got so infected they went in[to] shock and their kidneys shut down. A lot of them did die," he recalled. "It was really an awful situation. It touched me because I'd see young, [otherwise] healthy women in their twenties die from the consequences of an infected nonsterile abortion. Women would do anything to get rid of unwanted pregnancies. They'd risk their lives. It was a different world, I'll tell you."

"When I was at university in the '60s, abortion was completely illegal—and so was the dissemination of information about birth control. I remember my mother said that anybody who had money and a private doctor could get an abortion done, even back in the 1940s. But young women, poor women, working-class women—they could not. The injustice of that bothered me. A friend of mine got pregnant and asked if I knew a doctor who could help. Well, I didn't, but I've always had this quality of not accepting that I couldn't do things. So I helped her and found myself becoming part of a sort of underground referral network. I thought it was unjust that women had to suffer for no reason, when there was a safe procedure that could be done."

—Judy Rebick, *Canadian feminist and activist*

FIGHTING FOR CHANGE

Whenever there is oppression, there is resistance. And wherever abortion is illegal or inaccessible, there are people who will work hard—and sometimes take huge personal risks—to help women access safe abortions. In the United States and in Canada, many doctors risked their medical licenses and even prison sentences by defying the law and providing abortions. Other medical professionals, counselors and clergy helped women find their way to these safer—though still illegal—abortion providers. And women themselves organized and shared information. Word of mouth helped many women access safe abortions despite the law.

OUR BODIES, OURSELVES

OUR BODIES OUR SELVES
A COURSE BY AND FOR WOMEN

WOMEN UNITE

NEW PRINTING OF WOMEN & THEIR BODIES   35¢

The Boston Women's Health Book Collective began as a small group of women who were frustrated by the lack of information about their own bodies. They started meeting in 1969 and a year later published the first version of what would soon become the groundbreaking book Our Bodies, Ourselves. It provided straightforward information about sexuality and reproductive rights and health. The section on abortion begins: "Abortion is our right—our right as women to control our own bodies." The first edition, printed on newsprint, cost 75 cents. The book was reprinted in 1971—and word of mouth made it an underground success, selling 250,000 copies. Since then the book has been updated every few years, been translated into 30 languages and sold over four million copies.

The late 1950s saw the start of an intensely political time in North America. It was in 1955 that Rosa Parks refused to give up her seat on a bus to a white man in Montgomery, Alabama. Over the next decade the Civil Rights Movement fought for racial equality—battling against *segregation* and *discrimination*, and for full voting rights. By the late 1960s another political movement was beginning. People, many of them students, were demonstrating against the Vietnam War. In 1969 the gay, lesbian and transgender community fought back against police oppression in the Stonewall Riots, igniting the gay rights movement. And it was during this turbulent time that the **women's liberation movement** was born.

THE SECOND WAVE OF FEMINISM

The first wave of feminism had begun more than a 100 years earlier, during the mid-1800s, as women began demanding legal rights—in particular, the right to vote. The women's liberation movement of the 1960s and '70s was different. It focused on not just legal rights but also social attitudes and the often difficult truths of women's daily lives. Women began meeting in small groups—sometimes called consciousness-raising groups—to talk about their experiences. The idea that "the personal is political" became a rallying cry of the movement as people made connections between their own struggles and larger social structures, institutions and laws.

Feminists met in homes (above) and offices (below) to share their experiences and plan protests.

"It was such a political time; it was a time when the whole world seemed to be changing."
—Jackie Larkin, feminist, social justice activist

Demonstrators at a 1968 abortion rights protest in New York City.

One of the topics that women discussed in consciousness-raising groups was abortion. Many of them had had illegal abortions, and as they began speaking about these experiences—often for the first time—they discovered that they were not alone. Abortion rights began to be seen as an essential part of gender equality, and reproductive rights—both birth control and abortion—became a central focus for the women's liberation movement.

SAME PROCEDURE, DIFFERENT EXPERIENCES

When it comes to reproductive rights and freedoms, the histories and experiences of white women and women of color are very different. For example, one of the things that white women wanted in the 1960s and '70s was the right to access sterilization—to "get their tubes tied" to prevent future pregnancies. Doctors were reluctant to do this for white women unless they were older and had already had several children.

But during that same period, many hospitals ran programs in which women of color and Indigenous women were coerced or forced to undergo sterilization. One Indigenous organization, Women of All Red Nations, estimates that on some reserves in the United States, the rate of sterilization among women was as high as 80 percent. African American, Mexican and Puerto Rican women were also targeted by these campaigns. (Women with disabilities were—and still are—subjected to similar abuses—see page 129 for more information.) By 1968 a third of the women in Puerto Rico had been sterilized. So while white women wanted the right to access sterilization, women of color needed the right to refuse sterilization. Unfortunately, white feminist groups and mainstream pro-choice organizations often failed to recognize the different experiences and perspectives of women of color.

CHAPTER TWO

FIGHTING FOR CHOICE

Although women were fighting for change on both sides of the border, Canada and the United States had different histories—and different challenges—when it came to abortion rights, abortion access and public opinion.

THE FIGHT FOR LEGAL ABORTION
IN THE UNITED STATES

Pressure to change abortion laws in the United States came from many people. Women's organizations, doctors and the clergy all played important roles. As well as publicly advocating and fighting for change, all three groups also worked underground to help women access abortions more safely.

THE CLERGY CONSULTATION SERVICE
ON ABORTION

In 1967 Howard Moody, a Baptist minister at a New York City church, announced publicly that a group of Protestant and Jewish religious leaders would offer counseling and referrals for safe abortions. The Clergy Consultation Service on Abortion (CCS) grew,

Howard Moody, founder of the Clergy Consultation
Service on Abortion, in front of the Judson
Memorial Church in New York City's Greenwich
Village in 1967.

and by 1973 about 1,400 members of the clergy had helped hundreds of thousands of women access safe—though often illegal—abortions. Many of the clergy involved were people who had been active in the civil rights movement. They recognized that restrictions on abortion affected poor women and women of color far more than they did wealthy women and white women. They also saw a connection between their activism for racial justice and their commitment to helping women gain access to safe abortions.

Between 1967 and 1973, fourteen states made changes to their laws and began to allow women to access abortions in certain circumstances, such as if the pregnancy was considered life threatening. These abortions were referred to as ***therapeutic abortions***. In practice, this meant that women with money and connections could sometimes get legal abortions by finding a supportive doctor who was willing—for a fee—to say that a pregnancy was life threatening. Howard Moody and his colleague Arlene Carmen expressed

Arlene Carmen (left) and Howard Moody (right) around 1975. Between them is Al Carmines, a minister at Judson Memorial Church and a leading figure in experimental theater.

their frustration with this new law. "Therapeutic," they wrote in their book *Abortion Counseling and Social Change*, "was only a term to describe the difference between rich and poor, white and black, the privileged and the underprivileged, married and single."

Despite the efforts of the CCS, the cost of abortions—and the cost of travel to obtain them—remained a huge barrier. Thousands of women were still dying every year, and the majority of them were poor women of color. So in 1970, when New York State legalized abortion, the CCS partnered with a doctor and an administrator to open an abortion clinic that would provide affordable abortions in a supportive environment.

The Parents Aid Society (founded by activist Bill Baird) and members of the New York Radical Women group, demanding the legalization of abortion at a protest in front of the Rockefeller Center in New York City, in March 1968.

FEMINIST ORGANIZATIONS

Across the United States, feminist activists fought for reproductive freedom and advocated for changes in the law. Groups like the Redstockings held public "speak-outs," sharing their stories about getting illegal abortions or being forced to continue pregnancies. Their first speak-out, in New York's West Village on March 21, 1969, was attended by several hundred people. More abortion speak-outs soon followed in other cities across the country.

That same year, when legislators in New York sought advice from male experts, women stormed the hearing and insisted that their voices be heard. "We are the true experts, the only experts, we who've had abortions," one young woman told the legislative committee. And change began to happen, albeit slowly.

After New York and Hawaii legalized abortion, Washington, DC, Alaska and Washington State followed. American women who could afford to travel could now access legal abortions. For most women, though, traveling across the country to get an abortion was an impossibility, and illegal abortion rates remained high. Feminist organizations worked to provide practical support and loans. Across the United States, many women's groups formed to help women access illegal abortions more safely.

One of those groups was called the Abortion Counseling Service of Women's Liberation, but it soon became known as the Jane Collective, or Jane. Between 1969 and 1973, more than 100 women in Chicago joined the Jane Collective. The members made signs and posted them where women would see them. *Pregnant? Don't want to be? Call Jane.* They counseled women, gave them information and loaned them money to help them pay for the procedure.

But many of the doctors charged huge fees. Some were barely competent, and others treated their patients rudely. One was often drunk—and demanded sex as a condition for the abortion. When the members of Jane discovered that one of the abortion providers they were sending patients to didn't even have medical training, they decided to learn to perform abortions themselves. They performed around 11,000 abortions—and their safety record was similar to that of today's abortion clinics.

PREGNANT? DON'T WANT TO BE? CALL JANE AT 643-3844

A newspaper ad for the abortion-counseling service that became known as Jane.

JANE

RACHEL WILSON
ALLY SHWED

SINCE THE LATE 1970's, JUDITH ARCANA HAS WORKED WITH AND SPOKEN TO HUNDREDS OF WOMEN ON ANYTHING FROM FEMINISM TO TATTOOING...

...BUT WHATEVER THE TOPIC, THERE'S ALWAYS ONE QUESTION SHE GETS ASKED REPEATEDLY.

Do you think, um...

I was just wondering...

How do you manage to set up an illegal abortion service?

THIS IS BECAUSE, BETWEEN 1969 AND 1973, JUDITH AND OVER A HUNDRED OTHER WOMEN HELPED PROVIDE ACCESS TO ILLEGAL ABORTION SERVICES

OPERATING UNDER THE CODE NAME:

JANE
CHICAGO WOMEN'S ABORTION RIGHTS

OFFICIALLY KNOWN AS THE ABORTION COUNSELING SERVICE OF THE CHICAGO WOMEN'S LIBERATION UNION, JANE BEGAN SIMPLY AS A REFERRAL SERVICE.

There's a doctor we can get you in touch with.

BUT SOON IT BECAME A FEMINIST GROUP IN WHICH MEMBERS LEARNED TO PERFORM THE ABORTIONS **THEMSELVES.**

THEY WOULD PERFORM AN ESTIMATED 11,000 IN TOTAL BEFORE THEY FOLDED IN 1973, THE YEAR **ROE V. WADE** MADE ABORTION LEGAL IN ALL OF AMERICA.

GIVEN THE RELATIVELY LOW COST OF A JANE ABORTION, THE FRONT BECAME A **RARE POINT OF DIVERSITY** IN THE OTHERWISE WHITE, MIDDLE-CLASS LANDSCAPE OF WOMEN'S LIBERATION.

ANY WOMAN CAN BECOME PREGNANT WHO DOESN'T REALLY WANT TO BE. THERE WAS JUST AN ENORMOUS RESPECT FOR EVERYONE. —JEANNE GALATZER-LEVY

THERE WERE ONLY A FEW **WOMEN OF COLOR** IN JANE'S MEMBERSHIP AT ANY ONE TIME, AND **LOIS SMITH*** WAS ONE. IN AN INTERVIEW WITH LORETTA J. ROSS, SHE REMEMBERS: "WE COULD NEVER DEVELOP A CRITICAL MASS."

"BUT WE DIDN'T LOOK ON IT AS A **BLACK** OR **WHITE** WOMEN'S ISSUE; WOMEN NEEDED TERMINATION OF PREGNANCIES AND THERE WAS A _unity_ CREATED BY WOMEN WHO WERE DESPERATE."**

* PSEUDONYM
** SEE BIBLIOGRAPHY

I just can't afford another child.

My family will throw me out if I have a child out of wedlock.

I'm about to go to college. I can't have a child!

I just don't want children.

THERE WERE MANY REASONS FOR WOMEN TO SEEK ABORTIONS. JANE **NEVER** ASKED WHAT THE REASONS WERE — THEY JUST MADE SURE A WOMAN WAS CERTAIN SHE WANTED THE ABORTION AND WASN'T BEING FORCED INTO IT BY HER FAMILY OR PARTNER.

PRO-CHOICE DOCTORS

Doctors during this time were faced with a terrible choice. Helping women end their pregnancies meant risking their careers and facing possible imprisonment, but turning their backs on desperate patients meant being part of a system that often led to death and injury. Some doctors performed abortions despite the law. And some became vocal advocates for change.

Irving Goodman

Many doctors provided occasional abortions, secretly and illegally, when they couldn't bear to turn down a particularly distraught patient. And a few broke the law and provided abortions on a regular basis. One of these doctors was Irving Goodman. Born to Russian Jewish immigrants in 1926, he was raised in a family strongly committed to social justice. He also had personal reasons for wanting to help. When he and his future wife were teenagers in the 1940s, she became pregnant. They sought out an illegal abortion, which was a horrible and frightening experience. His girlfriend developed a serious infection from unsterilized instruments and needed surgery to save her life. On top of that, Irving Goodman's own mother had been orphaned at twelve when her mother died as a result of an illegal abortion. And like many others who have fought for abortion rights, he was also motivated by a concern about inequity: "It was definitely a political statement…because the rich could get (abortions). This was pissing me off, really. Because if you had enough money, I knew they could get the damn thing done."

"Those of us who were members of Jane were remarkable only because **we chose to act with women's needs as our guide.** In doing so we transformed an illegal abortion from a dangerous, sordid experience into one that was life-affirming and powerful. In the process, we ourselves were transformed."

—Laura Kaplan, in *The Story of Jane: The Legendary Underground Feminist Abortion Service*

Jane Hodgson

Despite the number of doctors who provided abortions illegally in the United States, only one was convicted: Jane Hodgson, of St. Paul, Minnesota. As a female OBGYN, she was flooded with requests for abortions. In the 1960s she began working with the

Jane Hodgson in 1989.

CCS to refer women to abortion providers outside the country or, when it became possible, to states with more relaxed abortion policies. But she knew many of her patients would seek out illegal abortions that put their lives at risk, and she became increasingly vocal about the need for safe, legal abortion. She said, "I had been taught that abortion was immoral...I came to feel that the law was immoral. There were all these young women whose health was being ruined, whose lives were being ruined."

In 1970 she decided to openly challenge the law. She spoke with a woman named Nancy Widmyer, who was pregnant and wanted an abortion. Nancy was in her twenties, married with three children and had been diagnosed with rubella (also known as German measles), which was known to cause potentially devastating injury to the fetus. Nancy agreed to help Jane Hodgson challenge the law. After visiting the federal court in Minnesota and requesting—unsuccessfully—that the law be **repealed**, Jane Hodgson scheduled Widmyer for an abortion at the hospital where she worked and performed the procedure. Shortly afterward, the police arrested her. Jane Hodgson was found guilty, but her conviction was later **overturned**, and she continued to be a vocal activist committed to women's reproductive freedom.

Marching for abortion rights shortly before the 1973 Supreme Court decision known as Roe v. Wade put an end to the illegal abortion era in the US.

ROE V. WADE

In 1973 the United States Supreme Court struck down all existing abortion laws in the famous decision known as *Roe versus Wade*, or *Roe v. Wade*. "Roe" referred to Jane Roe, the name the court used to refer to Norma Leah McCorvey, a twenty-one-year-old pregnant woman whose case represented all women who wanted abortions but could not get them legally and safely. "Wade" referred to Henry Wade, the Texas attorney general who defended the law that made abortion a crime. The Supreme Court ruled that Americans' right to privacy included the right of a woman to decide whether to have children, and the right of a woman and her doctor to make that decision without state interference.

Norma McCorvey (Jane Roe) and her lawyer, Gloria Allred, on the steps of the Supreme Court in 1989.

It was a landmark decision and a major victory for women. People who had been fighting for change were elated. But the battle wasn't over. Hospitals were slow to begin offering abortions after *Roe v. Wade*—and the court decision allowed states to place restrictions that effectively limited access to abortion, especially for young and poor women. And in the wake of *Roe v. Wade*, a **militant** and often fanatical anti-abortion movement began to organize—which you can read more about in chapter 3.

FIGHTING FOR CHOICE IN CANADA

During the 1960s and '70s activists in Canada were also fighting for change. Illegal abortion was common and often unsafe. Between 1926 and 1947, thousands of Canadian women died as a result of illegal abortions performed by incompetent providers.

By the 1960s, between 35,000 and 120,000 abortions were being performed every year. In 1963 the Canadian Medical Association started to lobby the government to change the abortion law. Women's organizations and social justice groups also began to advocate for change. And some doctors were already providing abortions, despite the risk of prosecution.

A protester at a subway station in Toronto, ON. Her sign is addressed to former Canadian prime minister Pierre Trudeau.

In 1967 Pierre Trudeau, then the justice minister, brought forward a bill that would allow abortion in certain circumstances. This bill also legalized contraception and *decriminalized* homosexuality. The bill was later passed as Bill C-150 and became law in 1969—100 years after abortion was first made a crime in Canada.

The law helped doctors, because it protected them from prosecution, but it did little to help women. Legal abortions could be performed only in hospitals, with the permission of three doctors. In bigger cities, hospitals formed Therapeutic Abortion Committees (TACs), which could approve an abortion if they believed the pregnancy endangered the woman's life or health. But most hospitals didn't have TACs, so women who lived outside big cities didn't have access to abortion. In those hospitals

In the fall of 1969 I was 19 and pregnant with a baby I did not want. Abortion had recently become legal in Canada, where I lived, so when I went to my doctor I was confident that my pregnancy would be terminated easily and safely. Not so. **He told me that the tribunal of doctors at my local hospital would never permit me to have a legal abortion and that he would not support my request.** Because I was young, healthy and hadn't been raped, I should just have the baby and make the best of it. He also told me that if I had an illegal abortion, I would risk becoming infertile and/or insane. I left his office enraged and never went back. Fortunately, my boss knew someone who put me in touch with an abortion provider in Vancouver, a ferry ride away. The cost was $500, which my boyfriend came up with.

The abortion was performed, illegally, in the doctor's office. The procedure was quick; the doctor and nurse were professional and supportive. I was given information about after-care, and I left via the back door, into an alley. I did develop an infection, but a few years later I was able to conceive and bear a much-wanted child. And I did not go insane.

I heard later that the doctor who had performed my abortion, and whose name I cannot remember, was arrested shortly after I visited him. All these years later I still wish I could tell him how much I admire what he did for me and countless other women and how grateful I am.

—Sarah Harvey, writer and editor

that had them, TACs often took up to two months to approve a procedure—by which time it might be too late for the woman to get an abortion. And while some TACs approved all requests automatically, others allowed very few abortions. In some cities, *anti-choice groups* began taking over hospital boards and stacking the TACs with anti-choice doctors.

DR. HENRY MORGENTALER

One doctor who disliked this new law was Henry Morgentaler, a Polish-born Canadian and a Holocaust survivor who had been imprisoned in a concentration camp during the Second World War. He graduated from medical school in Montreal and worked as a family doctor. After speaking out publicly to express his belief that women should be able to access safe, legal abortions, he began receiving numerous requests for help. At first he said no, explaining to the women that he could lose his job for helping them end their pregnancies. But after a while, knowing that women in Montreal were dying from unsafe abortions, he felt he could no longer turn them away. In 1968 he began performing abortions illegally as an act of *civil disobedience*. Five years later he announced that he had performed 5,000 abortions—outside hospitals and without the approval of a TAC. He also invited a television crew to film him doing an abortion; it was shown on national television.

Henry Morgentaler was arrested and tried three times by the provincial court of Quebec. In his defense he argued that his duty to protect the lives of the women who came to him outweighed his duty to obey the law. Some of his former patients gave testimony on his behalf. In each trial the jury found him not guilty. The jurors knew he had performed abortions, but they refused to enforce a law they felt was unjust.

freedom of choic

Dr. Henry Morgentaler speaks at a press conference in Ottawa, ON, in February 1976.

The judges were furious that juries were rebelling and refusing to enforce the law. So after the third acquittal, the Court of Quebec appealed the jury's decision—and five judges overturned the acquittal and replaced it with a conviction. Henry Morgentaler was sentenced to eighteen months in prison. He began serving his sentence in March 1975. While he was still in prison, the province laid a second set of charges against him—and he was acquitted by another jury. But he was still in jail. A political cartoon at the time showed a prison guard pushing Henry Morgentaler's food tray into his cell and saying, *"Congratulations, Doctor, you've been acquitted again!"*

The civil rights community fought back. A new federal law was passed, called the Morgentaler Amendment. This law prohibited courts from canceling a jury verdict. The government set aside Henry Morgentaler's wrongful conviction and ordered a new trial—and he was acquitted yet again. In the end he served ten months in jail. He had suffered a heart attack while in solitary confinement and was deeply in debt from his legal battles. But he never gave up. For Henry Morgentaler, this was only the beginning.

THE ABORTION CARAVAN

While Henry Morgentaler was fighting in the courts, feminist activists across the country were building an abortion rights movement, working to sway public opinion and pressure the government. In the spring of 1970 a small group of women set out from Vancouver, British Columbia, in a yellow Oldsmobile convertible, a Volkswagen bus and a pickup truck. They drove across the country, gathering women—and media attention— along the way.

The organizers called themselves the Vancouver Women's Caucus, and they were determined to put the issue of abortion on the national agenda. They reached out to other women's liberation groups across Canada, who organized events and rallies in their own communities. As the Abortion Caravan rolled through BC, Alberta, Saskatchewan, Manitoba and Ontario, momentum built.

In Ottawa signs went up: *THE WOMEN ARE COMING. ABORTION CARAVAN, MAY 9, 1:00 PM. PARLIAMENT HILL.* One of the Ottawa organizers was a young woman called Jackie Larkin, who was part of the Ottawa Women's Liberation group. Jackie says, "The Abortion Caravan tapped into this long deep history. All across the country, there were all these women who'd had illegal abortions and were ashamed about it. So as the caravan

In 1970 the women of the Abortion Caravan traveled to Ottawa, ON, where they protested on the lawn at the prime minister's residence, delivered a coffin to his front door and forced the House of Commons to shut down. They stood in front of the Parliament buildings, fists raised, calling for free abortion on demand.

drove through, and women heard about it, all these women came out and spoke about their experiences and gave testimonials. It was often the first time they'd ever spoken about their abortions."

Finally the Abortion Caravan arrived in Ottawa, and on Saturday, May 9, about 650 women and 50 men marched to Parliament Hill. At the head of the march, six women carried a black coffin to commemorate the deaths of the estimated 2,000 women who died each year from illegal abortions. The coffin had a coat hanger on top of it to symbolize the lives lost by those who attempted to end their own pregnancies.

But the prime minister, the justice minister and the health minister all refused to meet with the women. "We were pretty furious, because we felt we weren't getting the attention we deserved," Jackie remembers. "So we went outside and started to leave the hill—but instead of going back the way we came, we turned onto Sussex Drive and walked right to the prime minister's residence. Which they weren't expecting at all! We put the coffin right on his steps."

About 150 demonstrators from the Abortion Caravan held a sit-in at Prime Minister Pierre Trudeau's home, but still no government officials would agree to hear their concerns. *Pleas for Abortion Greeted By Silence* read the headlines in the *Ottawa Citizen*. Frustrated by the lack of response from government, the women held a strategy meeting that night. They decided that on Monday they would go into the House of Commons and disrupt Parliament.

We are programmed to believe that we can't change things and that it is foolish to even try. But... **ordinary women decided to rise up against a world that limited their possibilities**.

—Judy Rebick, in *Ten Thousand Roses: The Making of a Feminist Revolution*

Jackie recalls, "A sympathetic staffer got us passes to get into the gallery, but we had to find clothes—if we'd gone in our demonstration clothes, it would've been obvious we were up to something! So we were scrambling through closets to try to find skirts and nylons for everyone so that we could get into the House, and we had to find gloves to cover up the chains and handcuffs we were bringing in. So we all got our good clothes on and pretended we didn't know one another…and we spread out around the gallery. We chained ourselves to the seats so they couldn't remove us. And then at three o'clock we began shouting 'FREE ABORTION ON DEMAND!' One woman started the chant, and the rest of us gradually joined in. There were overhead mics that picked it up and amplified our voices, so they couldn't continue—they had to shut down the House for the first time ever."

Guards rushed in with wire cutters and hacksaws and dragged the protesters down the corridors and out a side entrance. Lynn Gibson, from Winnipeg, spoke to a reporter moments after she was thrown out of the building. "Few people seem to realize that women are being butchered by quack abortionists and are dying because of this present law," she said.

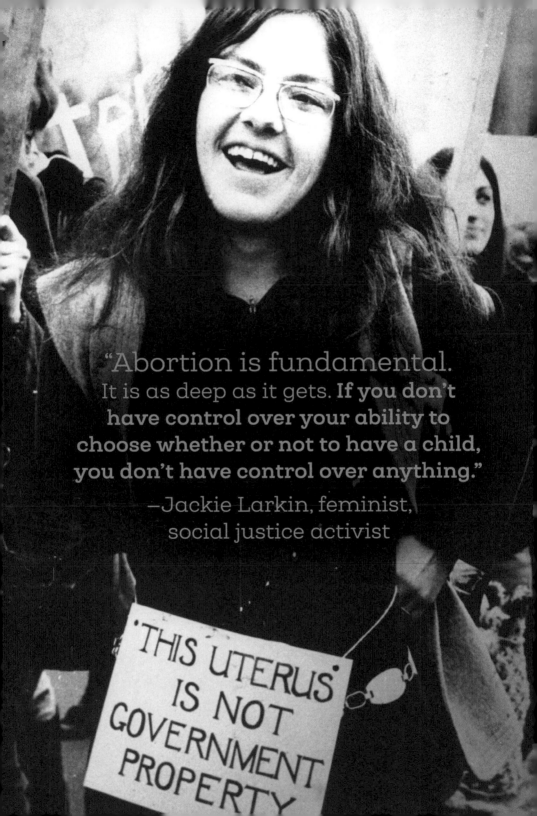

"Abortion is fundamental. It is as deep as it gets. **If you don't have control over your ability to choose whether or not to have a child, you don't have control over anything.**"

—Jackie Larkin, feminist, social justice activist

THIS UTERUS IS NOT GOVERNMENT PROPERTY

But that lack of awareness was about to change: the women had succeeded in getting the nation's attention. The next day newspapers across Canada made sure that people knew about the women's action and their cause. Abortion rights were now firmly on the national agenda, and much of the media was supportive. An editorial in the *Calgary Herald* argued, "We are advocating freedom. And this includes the freedom of a woman to decide what she does with her own body, to decide whether or not she shall bring a child into the world."

The Abortion Caravan remains one of the most extraordinary acts of civil disobedience in Canadian history.

BUILDING A MOVEMENT— AND WINNING THE BATTLE

Despite the success of the Abortion Caravan and the growing public support for abortion rights, women were still having to go through TACs to get abortions—and many women still couldn't access safe, legal abortions. The Canadian Association for the Repeal of the Abortion Law (CARAL) formed in 1974, and health-care workers in Toronto formed the Ontario Coalition for Abortion Clinics (OCAC) in 1982.

OCAC and CARAL decided to do what Henry Morgentaler had done in Quebec: set up a clinic, in violation of the law, and force change by taking the issue through the courts. Feminist and activist Judy Rebick went to the initial planning meeting—and found herself taking on a central role as the clinic's spokesperson.

In May 1983 Henry Morgentaler opened a clinic in Winnipeg. A month later it was raided by the police. Eight people, including Dr. Morgentaler, were arrested. The following month Morgentaler—with the help of OCAC and CARAL—established

We were fighting the government, the police, in the courts...But the juries were with us. The people were with us. The media was on our side. People recognized me. People on the subway would give me money for Morgentaler's defense fund. We were having big rallies and building support in different communities. **We really built a movement...and it just got bigger and bigger**.

—Judy Rebick, feminist and activist

an illegal abortion clinic in Toronto. But on the day the clinic officially opened, as Henry Morgentaler was being escorted from his taxi, a stranger jumped up and attacked him with a pair of garden shears. "I just jumped in and pulled him away," Judy Rebick says. "Why did I do that? Well, I was a fighter...And I fought back." Luckily, both Henry Morgentaler and Judy Rebick were uninjured.

The Toronto clinic was only open for three weeks before the government charged Dr. Morgentaler and two other doctors—Robert Scott and Leslie Smoling—under the abortion law. The police seized medical equipment and files, but the staff openly defied the authorities and reopened the clinic only minutes later. For Morgentaler it was the start of another long legal battle.

The following year all three doctors were found not guilty at a trial by jury. "The lawyer advised the jury that if they felt the law was unjust they could find Henry innocent—even though he was admitting that he was doing abortions, even though he was admitting that he was breaking the law," Judy Rebick explains. "The lawyer was very bold. He went after the law itself."

In 1985 the Ontario Court of Appeal ordered a new trial, arguing that Morgentaler's lawyer had told the jurors to ignore the law. Dr. Morgentaler appealed the order to the Supreme Court of Canada. While he was waiting for the Supreme Court decision, he was arrested again, on September 24, 1986, along with two other abortion providers, Nikki Colodny and Robert Scott. They continued to work, providing safe abortions to thousands

Judy Rebick and Dr. Henry Morgentaler outside the provincial courts in Toronto, ON, in January 1985.

of women despite ongoing arrests and harassment—and a deliberately set fire in the Women's Bookstore, which shared a building with the clinic.

And finally, in 1988—eighteen years after the Abortion Caravan—the Supreme Court handed down its ruling. The court found Canada's abortion law to be unconstitutional and in breach of Canada's Charter of Rights and Freedoms, which guarantees the right to life, liberty and security of the person.

Judy Rebick remembers that day vividly. "I was in front of the clinic the day the decision came down. I wasn't the spokesperson by that time, so I wasn't dressed to be on TV, but reporters kept

I had an abortion in February 1988 after forgetting to use contraception in a moment of passion. It was not a hard decision, as I never wanted kids. I got my abortion approved under the old 'therapeutic abortion' regime, although luckily I didn't have to appear before a committee. It was Vancouver General Hospital, and they just rubber-stamped all applications. But **I still couldn't believe I had to apply for permission. It was shocking and enraging.** I had to wait three weeks, and that was very hard because I was sick and miserable...I felt very happy after my abortion and was greatly relieved to get my normal life back.

—Joyce Arthur, executive director, Abortion Rights Coalition of Canada

saying *Just tell us how you feel*, and I just jumped into the air and said, *I feel great!* I felt more joy in that moment than ever before. The joy of winning that battle—and it was a real battle. There was violence, there were death threats, and a guy even tried to throw me off a subway platform. It was a real battle and a real victory, and we worked and fought hard for it. And it wasn't easy."

This wasn't the end—there were still challenges ahead. In 1990 the government introduced a bill that would have again criminalized many abortions—and it was passed in the House of Commons before being narrowly defeated in the Senate. And threats to funding have continued to limit access in parts of the country. However, the Supreme Court decision was—and remains—a tremendous victory.

Today Canada has no law restricting abortion. "And we've been doing just fine without it," activist Joyce Arthur says. "We've found that doctors and women exercise the right to abortion responsibly, without the need for any legal restrictions. We don't need **gestational limits**. We don't need waiting periods. We don't need parental- or spousal-consent laws. And we don't need restrictions on certain types of abortions."

Activist Joyce Arthur at the mic at an abortion rights protest in Canada. The protesters are dressed as handmaids in a reference to The Handmaid's Tale, a novel by Margaret Atwood that depicts a world in which women have been stripped of all rights and forced to bear children. Handmaid costumes have been used in protests across North America.

THE ABORTION RIGHTS COALITION OF CANADA

About six months after her own abortion during Canada's era of therapeutic abortion committees, Joyce Arthur came across a pro-choice rally at the Vancouver Art Gallery. Despite feeling shy and unsure, she signed up to be a volunteer for the group that organized it: the BC Coalition for Abortion Clinics. A few years later she found herself leading the group. And in 2005, after CARAL closed down, Joyce founded the Abortion Rights Coalition of Canada (ARCC) with support and participation from advocates across the country.

Today Joyce is the executive director of ARCC, which works to protect and improve access to reproductive health services, especially abortion, across Canada. "The right to abortion is really a bedrock human right," Joyce says, "because if you can't control your fertility, you don't have control over your life or body. You cannot fully exercise other rights if you don't control when and whether you have children."

CHAPTER THREE

ABORTION UNDER ATTACK

After the *Roe v. Wade* decision made abortion legal across the United States, people who were opposed to legal abortion immediately began working to undermine the new law. They couldn't attack it directly—the Supreme Court is the highest court there is, so they couldn't appeal the decision. Instead they worked to make abortions more difficult to get. Since 1973 their strategies have included lobbying state governments, making financial contributions to anti-choice politicians and bringing forward legal challenges. As a result, many states have passed numerous laws that restrict access to abortion.

Anti-choice activists have also mounted a **propaganda** campaign that involves the spreading of outright lies and misinformation about abortion. And some have engaged in harassment and even violence. They refer to themselves as "pro-life"—but show little concern for the lives of people facing unwanted pregnancies. In fact, the states that have the most extreme record of attacking reproductive rights also have the worst health outcomes for women and children, and the fewest policies that support the well-being of families.

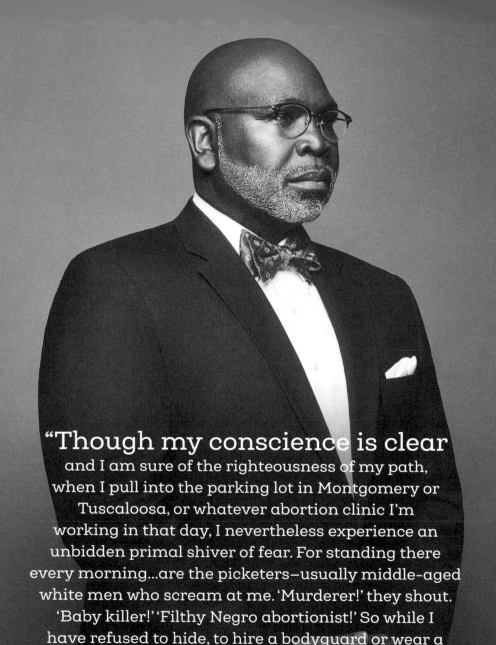

"**Though my conscience is clear**
and I am sure of the righteousness of my path,
when I pull into the parking lot in Montgomery or
Tuscaloosa, or whatever abortion clinic I'm
working in that day, I nevertheless experience an
unbidden primal shiver of fear. For standing there
every morning...are the picketers—usually middle-aged
white men who scream at me. 'Murderer!' they shout.
'Baby killer!' 'Filthy Negro abortionist!' So while I
have refused to hide, to hire a bodyguard or wear a
bulletproof vest, it's impossible to escape these thoughts:
People have been assassinated for what you do.
This could be your last day."

—Dr. Willie Parker, in *Life's Work:*
A Moral Argument for Choice

In Canada, too, anti-abortion groups began to form—and in 1975 a petition against abortion rights, with more than one million signatures, was delivered to Parliament. While many people who oppose abortion rights express their views in legal and peaceful ways, others are far more confrontational. Tactics used by Canadian anti-abortion groups are often directly copied from those used by the much larger anti-abortion movement in the United States.

These groups who oppose abortion don't do anything for day care or social services or prenatal care; they cut affordable care and maternity care. **They don't care about any of that: none of their actions are congruent with concern for the lives of women or babies.**

–Françoise Girard, president of the International Women's Health Coalition (IWHC)

VIOLENCE AND HARASSMENT

During the 1980s, an increasingly militant anti-abortion movement began attacking abortion clinics and providers. They demonstrated in front of clinics, harassing women who were seeking abortions and attempting to block their access. They threatened doctors and staff and vandalized clinics.

Anti-abortion groups referred to abortion as murder, fanning the flames of *fanaticism*, and the level of violence escalated. Highly organized groups bombed clinics and attacked doctors, nurses and clinic staff.

In 1992 Dr. Morgentaler's clinic in Toronto was destroyed by a bomb. The following year, Florida doctor David Gunn became the first abortion provider murdered by an anti-abortion extremist. Over the next fifteen years a number of doctors, clinic escorts, receptionists and nurses were injured or killed. Anti-abortion extremists from the United States crossed the border into Canada, and three Canadian abortion providers, in British Columbia,

Manitoba and Ontario, were shot in their own homes. Luckily all three doctors survived, but in 1998 another abortion provider, Barnett Slepian, was shot and killed in his home in Buffalo, New York. The man convicted of his murder was also charged with one of the shootings in Canada and is thought to have been responsible for the others. In 2009 George Tiller—who had already survived the firebombing of his clinic in 1986 and being shot in both arms in 1993—was murdered by an anti-abortion extremist while serving as an usher at his church in Kansas.

The events were devastating to the families and communities directly affected, to abortion providers who had to live with the fear of violence, and to everyone who cared about women's health and reproductive justice. But while some young doctors may have been discouraged from providing abortions due to fears about their safety, others began to organize and fight back.

DR. GARSON ROMALIS

Dr. Garson Romalis, the Canadian physician introduced in the previous chapter, survived two murder attempts. He had been practicing medicine for more than 30 years when he was shot through the window of his own home in 1994. He had a severe gunshot wound and almost died. After about two years of rehabilitation he returned to work, including providing abortion services. Six years later he was stabbed as he entered the clinic where he worked. Luckily his injuries were minor. After two months he returned to the practice of medicine—and restricted his practice to providing abortions. He said, "It is still hard for me to understand how someone could think I should be killed for helping women get safe abortions...These acts of terrorist violence have affected virtually every aspect of my and my family's life. Our lives have changed forever." But his views on abortion and his commitment to women's health remained unchanged, and he continued providing abortions until he died in 2014, at age 76, after a brief illness.

"It's easier to strip us of our rights when we're not treated as humans, when political candidates say we deserve 'some form of punishment,' when elected officials vote to define abortion as 'murder,' when people call us killers. **Language matters, and it leads to violence.** Abortion providers and people who share their stories, including me, have received thousands of threats."

—Renee Bracey Sherman, founder of We Testify, a program of the National Network of Abortion Funds

MEDICAL STUDENTS FOR CHOICE

Medical Students for Choice (MSFC) is a student organization that started in 1993. It originally formed in response to David Gunn's murder and to other actions by anti-abortion groups. MSFC works to make sure that medical students can get the training they need

For more than 25 years, the group Medical Students for Choice has been working to create tomorrow's abortion providers and pro-choice physicians.

to do abortions. Despite the fact that abortion is one of the most common medical procedures, it is not taught to most medical students.

"We have many people in positions of authority in medical schools and the community who are anti-choice," says Joyce Arthur, executive director of the Abortion Rights Coalition of Canada. "They want to maintain the silence and stigma around abortion." When future doctors are not educated on abortion and family planning, they can't offer their patients a full range of health care services. MSFC has more than 10,000 members at over 210 medical schools around the world— and this student-led organization has made it possible for thousands of future doctors to receive abortion education and training.

CLINIC ESCORTS

In places where abortion clinics have been targeted by protesters, volunteers have organized to support and protect patients. Clinic escorts keep an eye on picketers and report them if they are in violation of the law. Some states, provinces and municipalities have specific laws requiring protesters to stay outside a "buffer zone," "bubble zone" or "access zone." Often wearing brightly

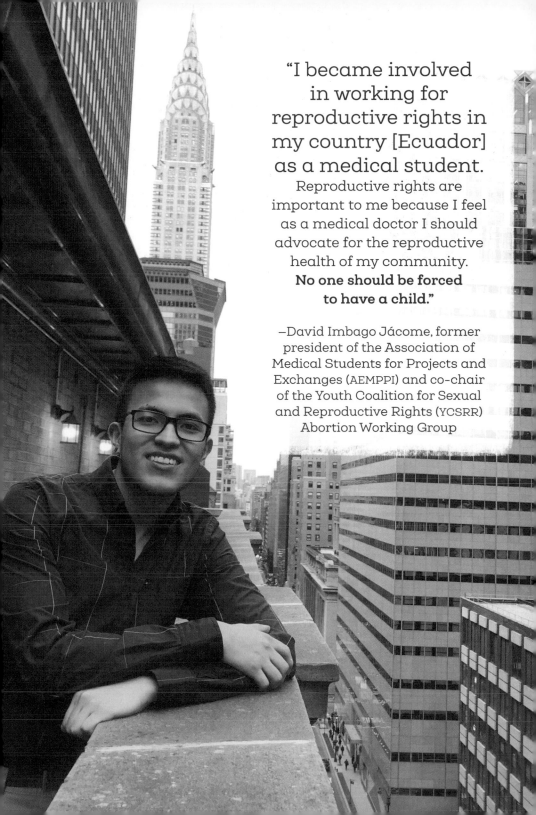

"I became involved in working for reproductive rights in my country [Ecuador] as a medical student. Reproductive rights are important to me because I feel as a medical doctor I should advocate for the reproductive health of my community. **No one should be forced to have a child.**"

—David Imbago Jácome, former president of the Association of Medical Students for Projects and Exchanges (AEMPPI) and co-chair of the Youth Coalition for Sexual and Reproductive Rights (YCSRR) Abortion Working Group

These clinic escorts from the Illinois Choice Action Team are also board members of the Clinic Vest Project, a nonprofit organization that sends free clinic-escort vests to groups in the United States, Canada and the UK. The Clinic Vest Project was started in 2013 by reproductive rights activist Benita Ulisano (left).

colored vests, clinic escorts welcome people visiting the clinic, ensure that protesters are not blocking their entry and, when necessary, physically escort patients through an intimidating and often hostile crowd. Their work is not without danger. Escorts may face harassment and threats of violence, and one clinic escort, James Barrett, was shot to death outside a clinic in Florida.

RESTRICTIONS TO ACCESS IN THE UNITED STATES

After *Roe v. Wade*, states appealed to the Supreme Court of the United States dozens of times, seeking to limit access to abortion, but for the most part the Supreme Court rejected these attempts and enforced *Roe v. Wade*'s ruling. However, the court handed down two important rulings that seriously limited access for young women and poor women. In 1979 the Supreme Court ruled that states could require a minor to either obtain parental consent or persuade a judge that she was mature enough to make her own decision. And in 1980 the Supreme Court upheld the Hyde Amendment, which limited access to abortion for women who depended on Medicaid for health insurance.

The Hyde Amendment was first introduced in 1976, just three years after *Roe v. Wade*, and has been the subject of numerous legal challenges. It bans federal funding from being used for abortion coverage except in rare circumstances (for example, if a woman's life is in danger). Each US state is bound by the federal constitution but also by its own state constitution—and in sixteen states, reproductive rights advocates have succeeded in ensuring that state funds can be used to pay for abortions even though the federal Medicaid program does not help cover this cost.

Demonstrators in Washington, DC, rally in support of reproductive rights on International Women's Day in 2017.

In those states, low-income people do have abortion coverage under their state Medicaid programs. In other states, however, the cost of abortion is not covered. People with low incomes and whose insurance will not cover abortion struggle to find the hundreds of dollars they need to pay for the procedure. For many of these people it may mean missing a rent payment or not buying groceries. Others will have later abortions, and some will be forced to carry their pregnancy to term and deliver a baby—even if this poses a threat to their own health. For more than forty years the Hyde Amendment has made abortion unaffordable for millions of Americans. In 2017 the US government passed a bill making the Hyde Amendment permanent.

MANDATORY WAITING PERIODS

Many states require patients to have a pre-abortion counseling session and then wait for up to three days before having an abortion. This means they have to make two trips to the clinic, which is especially difficult for people who live far from their nearest abortion provider. They have to take time off work twice. Find childcare twice. Pay for travel costs twice. All the difficulties of accessing an abortion are doubled. Almost no other medical procedure requires a waiting period. This is a

SPEAKING OUT

I was 22, about to graduate from college with a 4.0 GPA and an acceptance letter into my top choice for graduate school when I found out that I was pregnant. Immediately, I knew I wanted an abortion. **I remember being so frustrated that I needed to make two appointments because I couldn't have the procedure the same day due to Ohio's mandatory delay requirement.** The day that I walked into Planned Parenthood for my appointment, four white men were standing outside shouting at me. Even my boyfriend called me selfish and tried to talk me out of making the decision every chance he had. Luckily, I had a gang of friends who were on my side. People who had abortions were there to assure me that everything was going to be okay—and it was. When I walked out of the health center after having my abortion, for the first time in my life, I felt like I had power.

–Kersha Deibel, from We Testify: Our Abortion Stories

medically unnecessary requirement that exists solely to make it harder for people to get abortions.

Research shows that waiting periods do not lower the abortion rate—they merely make abortions more difficult to get. They cause emotional stress for people seeking abortions, the vast majority of whom are already clear about their decision to end the pregnancy by the time they make an appointment. They also cause delays, as people may need time to raise the extra funds required to make the trip twice. This in turn may increase the number of abortions performed later in pregnancy. Although abortion is very safe, the risk of complications increases as the pregnancy progresses. The cost of the procedure also increases, which causes real difficulties for those who are poor: if you have to take time to raise the funds for an abortion, you are more likely to have an abortion later, which will cost even more.

All restrictions to abortion access hurt those living in poverty. Groups that are already *marginalized*—such as women of color and women with disabilities—tend to be the most negatively affected.

PARENTAL CONSENT AND NOTIFICATION LAWS

The number of teen pregnancies is declining with higher rates of contraceptive use. Still, more than 400,000 American teens become pregnant every year. Most of those pregnancies are unplanned, and nearly a third of them end in abortion. However, some of these teens will not find it easy to access abortion services, because people under eighteen are targeted by abortion restrictions. The majority of US states require that either one or both parents consent to a minor's abortion or that parents be notified before the abortion takes place.

In fact, most teens who have abortions choose to tell their parents—and the younger the teen, the more likely they are to discuss this decision with at least one of their parents. Many teens who don't talk to a parent do talk to another adult they trust. But studies have shown that when teens do not want to involve their parents, they usually have good reasons. They may fear physical abuse or being kicked out of the house, they may have a difficult family situation, or they may not even be living with parents.

Parental consent laws can also put teens at risk by discouraging them from seeking medical care at all, making it more likely that an abortion will need to be done later in the pregnancy and increasing the risk that teens might obtain an illegal abortion or attempt to end the pregnancy on their own. When a state requires

Some states require teens to get permission from one or both parents to have an abortion. Other states don't require permission but do say that the teen's parents will have to be notified. You can find an up-to-date list of parental consent and notification laws on Planned Parenthood's website.

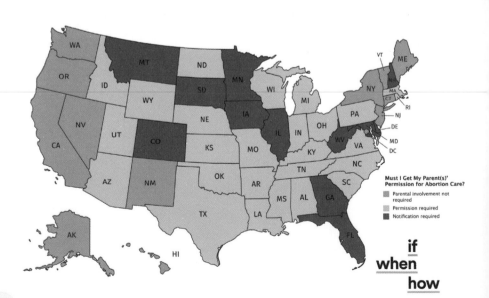

Must I Get My Parent(s)'
Permission for Abortion Care?

Parental involvement not required

Permission required

Notification required

if
when
how

parents to be involved, some teens will travel to get abortions in states that have fewer restrictions.

Teens in states that have parental consent or notification laws can go to court to request a waiver of the requirement to notify parents: this is called a *judicial bypass*. But many teens are too scared to talk to a judge about something so private. And even if they do, obtaining a judicial bypass can take several weeks, which leads to stress and anxiety—and later abortions.

Stephanie Pineiro experienced the challenges of judicial bypass firsthand. She was seventeen years old, Latina and a first-generation college student working multiple jobs to help support her family. When her summer romance began at the pizza shop where she worked, "it blossomed into my first taste of true love,"

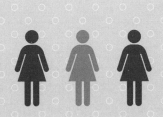

One in three Janes does not live with a parent or a legal guardian.

This means there is **no one** in her life who can legally consent to her abortion.

From JDP's 2016 Impact Report

In Texas, Jane's Due Process works to ensure legal representation for minors. To protect their confidentiality, teens who apply for judicial bypasses are referred to as Jane Does—or Janes for short.

Stephanie recalls. Stephanie's Catholic pediatrician refused to give her birth control, telling her that her parents would find out and that God didn't want her having sex so young. So when the couple started having sex, they relied on condoms.

"At the end of the summer, the condom broke," she explains. Stephanie and her boyfriend researched options online and found out about emergency contraception—also known as plan B or the morning-after pill. Stephanie's boyfriend was eighteen, so he went to the pharmacy to buy the pill that could prevent a potential pregnancy. But the pharmacist refused to sell it to him, and Stephanie spent the next two weeks waiting, wondering and searching online for information on ways to end the pregnancy herself. She googled *DIY abortion* and *How to cause a miscarriage*

Stephanie Pineiro in September 2017 at Capitol Hill Advocacy Day. Young advocates traveled there to meet with senators, share their stories and lobby for reproductive rights.

and even considered having someone push her down the stairs. Two weeks later she took a pregnancy test in the bathroom at work. It was positive.

"I left work and drove straight to the college I was attending and waited for my boyfriend to get out of class. We needed to talk," Stephanie recalls. "I told him I was pregnant. It was his second year of college, and he wanted to transfer to a big university to play football. I was in dual enrollment with big dreams to become a lawyer. We couldn't do this. We didn't want this. We needed to live our lives on our own terms."

Stephanie researched her options and learned about judicial bypass. She found a hotline, and after two days of trying to get through, she was given contact details for an attorney who would take her case. "A day later I was in her office. The attorney told me I needed to gather evidence showing the judge it would be unsafe if I told my parents I was having an abortion. As the aspiring lawyer I was, I took on the challenge and decided to go beyond what the attorney asked for and prove to the judge his decision wouldn't be made in vain. I brought my newly minted college transcript, wrote a five-page essay and provided legal documentation highlighting instances of the domestic violence my family and I suffered."

Stephanie had made her attorney's case easy, but the next step was a frightening one. "My fate was put in the hands of a judge," she says. "I was scared. I was confused. I was alone. The only thing that kept me going was my survival instinct kicking into gear. I knew that I'd figure it out—I had to. I always did.

A week later Stephanie got her hearing. "I don't remember what I said or if it even mattered," she explains. "It must've been compelling, since the next day I received my court order that called me Jane Doe. I told my parents I was going to school and was at the clinic first thing in the morning. I stayed until the clinic closed, and my boyfriend dropped me off at my car so I could drive home. I walked back into my parents' house and helped my mom peel potatoes for dinner."

Because of her own experience, Stephanie became a committed and passionate advocate for reproductive rights. She is now the board vice-president of the Central Florida Women's Emergency Fund, a group that provides financial support to people who are trying to get abortions, and she speaks publicly about her own experience of abortion as a We Testify storyteller.

"I was lucky to have been granted a judicial bypass, and I know this is not the reality for many teens around the country," she says. "I hope you know I fight for you every day. I see you. I feel you. You are not alone, and you deserve better than what this system is offering you. Demand better and fight for what you need."

TRAP LAWS

Many states have passed Targeted Regulation of Abortion Providers (TRAP) laws, which focus on clinics that provide abortions. While all medical facilities are subject to health and safety requirements, TRAP laws impose requirements on abortion providers that are not imposed on other medical providers and often have nothing to do with patient health and safety. At the time of this writing, twenty-four states had laws or policies that regulate abortion providers. These policies go far beyond what is necessary to protect patients. Some TRAP laws dictate the size of janitor's closets or clinic parking spaces, or require health centers to keep the grass outside cut to a certain height. The goal of these unnecessary and expensive regulations is to force abortion clinics to close—and in some cases this strategy has been successful.

Most of these clinic closures have been in the South, where more than half of Black Americans live. Many counties have no abortion clinics. Five states have only one. In a 2014 survey of abortion patients in the United States, three-quarters of those surveyed said that they were having an abortion because they could not afford to raise a child, yet the states in which abortions are hardest to get are also the ones where women are most likely to live in poverty. Again, poor women and women of color are most affected by these laws.

ANTI-ABORTION PROPAGANDA

One of the strategies used by those who oppose abortion involves attempting to influence public opinion by making abortion seem much less safe than it actually is. Anti-abortion activists spread false information that directly contradicts scientific evidence about abortion—and this misinformation is often directly targeted at young people and people who are facing unwanted pregnancies.

ABSTINENCE-ONLY EDUCATION

Much false information is actively taught within the US school system. Many states have *abstinence-only education programs*—sexual-education programs that teach students not to have sex until marriage. These programs often exaggerate the failure rates of such contraceptives as condoms, birth control pills and IUDs, provide false information about HIV and sexually transmitted infections, and perpetuate myths about abortion. They do not teach sexually active teens about safer sex or provide information about how to avoid pregnancy.

MY BODY. MY CHOICE

Pro-Freedom. Pro-Justice. Pro-Choice. NARAL PRO-CHOICE AMERICA WWW.PROCHOICEAMERICA.ORG

I REPRO

87% of fake women's health centers lie to wom who walk through the do

In March 2018 activists rallied in front of the Supreme Court of the United States as part of the #EndTheLies campaign to draw attention to the deceptive practices of crisis pregnancy centers.

Studies have found that abstinence-only sex education has little or no impact on rates of abstinence. In other words, telling teenagers not to have sex doesn't actually influence whether they have sex or not. However, there is one area in which abstinence-only sex programs *do* have an impact: the rates of teen pregnancy. The states with abstinence-only programs have the highest rates of teen pregnancy. Not surprisingly, teenagers who receive comprehensive sex education are significantly less likely to get pregnant.

CRISIS PREGNANCY CENTERS

Crisis pregnancy centers are another source of misinformation in both the United States and Canada. These centers, which outnumber abortion clinics by three to one, advertise themselves as counseling centers or medical clinics—places that offer support, resources and options. They often receive public funds. But rather than being supported in making their own choices, clients are given misinformation that greatly exaggerates the risks of abortion and seeks to persuade them to continue their pregnancies. While they may provide some useful services, these clinics often have an anti-abortion agenda that relies on manipulating and lying to their clients. The Abortion Rights Coalition of Canada examined the websites of Canadian crisis pregnancy centers and published its findings in 2016. The report showed that most centers have websites that spread misleading or inaccurate information about abortion, contraception, sexually transmitted infections, sexual activity and adoption. Many also hide their religious affiliations and are not up-front about the fact that they won't help people access abortions.

The first place we went to was one of those horrible places that shows you aborted-fetus pictures and tries to shame you into keeping the child: a crisis pregnancy center. After that traumatic experience, we found a Planned Parenthood clinic that would do the procedure and a few days later, went in and thankfully had people who understood the decision we'd made.

—Tanya DePass, from We Testify: Our Abortion Stories

MISINFORMED CONSENT

Some states require doctors to read informed-consent scripts aloud to their patients before providing an abortion. For any medical procedure, **informed consent** is an important concept. Patients need to be given appropriate information so that they understand all their options, are aware of any risks and can make good decisions about their care. Abortion providers support this.

But in many US states, specific laws dictate the scripts that abortion providers must read—and in the majority of those states, these scripts are heavily influenced by anti-abortion **ideology**

MYTHS & FACTS
ABOUT ABORTION

Myth: Having an abortion is dangerous for your health.

FACT: The risks of continuing a pregnancy and delivering a baby are approximately 10 times higher than the risks of an abortion during the first trimester of a pregnancy.

Myth: Abortion increases your risk of breast cancer.

FACT: There is good scientific evidence that abortion does not increase your risk of breast cancer.

Myth: People who have abortions often regret the decision and experience depression afterward.

FACT: An unplanned pregnancy can be a stressful experience. Most people who have abortions feel relieved afterward. It is true that some people who choose to end an unplanned pregnancy will experience difficulties and depression afterward. But so will some people who choose to continue the pregnancy. Choosing an abortion does not lead to a higher risk of depression than choosing to continue an unplanned pregnancy.

Myth: Having an abortion makes it difficult to get pregnant in the future.

FACT: A safe, legal and uncomplicated first-trimester abortion has no effect on future fertility.

Myth: Fetuses experience pain during abortions.

FACT: Fetuses cannot feel pain until at least the 24th week of pregnancy.

and propaganda. Doctors are required to tell patients that the procedure poses various risks to their future physical and mental health—for example, informing them that infertility is a risk of abortion even though scientific evidence shows this to be untrue.

Some doctors deal with this by telling their patients that though they are required to read the information to them, studies have shown it to be false. Willie Parker, an abortion provider in the southern states, says, "In Mississippi, I am required to inform women that having an abortion increases their risk for breast cancer, a fraudulent fact—a lie!—for which no scientific evidence exists; I tell them what the law requires and then, in the same breath, I explain to these women that it's simply not true."

It is important for people to have accurate information about their bodies and choices, and it is essential for those people who support reproductive rights to be able to challenge these lies when they encounter them.

CHOICE AND THE CHURCH

One very powerful and vocal lobby group that opposes abortion rights is the Catholic Church. Countries that are strongly influenced by Catholic ideology generally have laws banning or heavily restricting abortion, and sometimes also limiting access to contraception. At the international level, the Catholic Church has done a great deal to undermine reproductive rights. Despite being no larger than a golf course and having only a few hundred citizens— less than fifty of whom are women—Vatican City is represented as a state at the United Nations. Its government, the Holy See, has used its status at the UN to impose its views on whole populations, Catholic and non-Catholic alike. Finding allies in conservative countries like Russia, Iran and Saudi Arabia, the Vatican has

Catholics for Choice standing up for abortion rights at the United States Supreme Court building in Washington, DC.

repeatedly blocked efforts to protect the reproductive rights and freedoms of women and girls around the world.

Despite the official position of the church, Catholics are just as likely to have abortions as non-Catholics. The large majority of Catholics reject the church's teaching and embrace contraception: a 2015 poll in the United States found that 86 percent felt it was "morally acceptable." And many—in some countries, most—Catholics do not agree with the official position of the Catholic Church on abortion. Groups like Catholics for Choice are working toward change.

REPRODUCTIVE RIGHTS AND THE TRUMP-PENCE ADMINISTRATION

Since the inauguration of President Donald Trump in 2017, the future of reproductive choice in the United States has felt more uncertain than it has in many years. During his election campaign Trump stated that there should be "some form of punishment" for women having abortions—and his choice of Mike Pence as vice-president sent a clear and chilling message. Pence has pushed extreme anti-choice bills, including one that would have required women to hold funerals for fetal tissue and another that would have allowed Catholic hospitals to refuse to do abortions even when necessary to save a woman's life. And he has vowed to "send *Roe v. Wade* to the ash heap of history, where it belongs."

Only the Supreme Court can overturn *Roe v. Wade*—and Donald Trump has promised to fill any vacancies with "pro-life" judges who will do just that. In 2017 he appointed Neil Gorsuch, and in 2018, despite sexual-assault allegations against him, Brett Kavanaugh was also confirmed. These two judges tip the balance of the Supreme Court to a conservative majority that could directly overturn—or effectively gut—*Roe v. Wade*. Trump has also nominated many deeply conservative judges to the lower courts—and most of these appointments are for life. The impact of these judges' decisions will be felt by millions of Americans for decades to come.

Encouraged by the Trump administration, many states have introduced hundreds of anti-abortion bills, including some outright bans that directly contradict the right to abortion guaranteed by *Roe v. Wade*. Although these bills are immediately challenged in court by reproductive rights advocates, they are part of an effort to bring a bill before a more conservative Supreme Court that could overturn *Roe v. Wade*. If this happens, abortion rights in the United States will be up to individual states. Whether people can get abortions will depend on where they live—and whether they can afford to travel to another state to get the procedure done.

Reproductive rights activists outside
the Supreme Court of the United States
(SCOTUS).

The Trump–Pence administration has placed anti-choice advocates in key government positions—and new attacks on reproductive rights are happening constantly. In 2018 the administration announced a move to place restrictions on Planned Parenthood (which Mike Pence has been trying to defund for many years) and other health providers that receive federal funding for family planning and reproductive health care. This will make it more difficult for doctors to refer patients to abortion providers and may mean that patients are less likely to get full and accurate information about their care options. This policy is being called a "domestic gag rule," and it could impact millions of people who rely on Planned Parenthood and other affected health-care providers.

Undermining such health providers makes it harder for people to access contraception and routine health screening. And federal funding aimed at reducing teen pregnancy is being shifted away from comprehensive sex education to abstinence-based education—which research shows is linked to higher teen pregnancy rates. So at the same time that this administration is attacking reproductive choice and abortion rights, it is also pursuing policies likely to lead to more unwanted pregnancies.

While the threat this administration poses is very real, so is the powerful resistance that has been mobilized. "The silver lining is that we have a really powerful organizing tool for 2020," says Destiny Lopez, the co-director of All* Above All, a network of reproductive rights advocates. "The election really brought a daunting challenge to our doorstep, but we women—low-income people, people of color, immigrants—we are used to fighting against impossible odds."

CHAPTER FOUR

FIGHTING FOR SAFE ABORTION AROUND THE WORLD

A round the world, one in every four pregnancies ends in an abortion—and almost half of those abortions are unsafe. That is 25 million unsafe abortions every year. Instead of being performed by well-trained doctors in clinics or hospitals, they are done by unqualified people in unsterile conditions. All too often they result in injury, infection or death.

The large majority of unsafe abortions—97 percent—occur in developing countries in Africa, Asia and Latin America.

Illegal and unsafe abortion takes a devastating toll on women's lives and health. Globally, an estimated 47,000 women die from complications of unsafe abortion each year, and almost all of these deaths occur in developing countries. A woman dies of complications from unsafe abortion every eight minutes—and every year these deaths leave 220,000 children motherless.

The rate of injury and illness caused is far higher. Every year around seven million women in developing countries are treated for complications from unsafe abortions. Millions more experience complications but never receive treatment. Many women are left with lifelong health problems.

Of course, it is not just in developing countries that women are unable to access abortion. Many developed countries also criminalize abortion. In Poland, for example, abortion is banned except in cases of rape or incest or when the health of the mother or fetus is at serious risk. In Northern Ireland, abortion is even more restricted: it's against the law unless the pregnancy endangers the life of the woman. And in South Korea, abortion was illegal but commonly performed until late 2009, when the government began enforcing the law because of concern about the declining birth rate in the country. Some women are able to travel to another country to access abortion services. But most women

AFRICAN COUNTRIES, EUROPEAN LAWS

Before Africa was colonized by Europeans, abortion was generally regarded as a private matter, and abortions were provided by traditional practitioners. Anti-abortion laws in most African countries are a legacy of **colonialism**—that is, they were passed by the governments of the European countries that occupied the continent. Many of these laws are still in place, causing tremendous suffering to millions of women. In Sierra Leone, for example, the law that criminalizes abortion was passed by the British and has been in effect since 1861. In Nigeria, another former British colony, abortion is a criminal offense unless deemed necessary to save a woman's life, and is punishable by jail time for both the abortion provider and the woman ending her pregnancy.

People sometimes assume that laws that prohibit abortion or highly restrict access to it will lower the abortion rate. But there is clear evidence that this is not the case at all. In fact, the opposite is true. Countries where abortion is illegal actually have slightly higher rates of abortion than do countries where abortion is available on demand. This may seem surprising—but in many countries that restrict or prohibit abortion, women also have limited access to contraception. In developing countries, an estimated 214 million women need modern contraceptives and are not able to get them. Abortion rates are always higher when women are not able to prevent unwanted pregnancies.

cannot afford to pay thousands of dollars for travel and medical care.

The problem may seem overwhelming, but there is a strong and growing global movement working toward change. In 2015 the United Nations agreed on a set of goals to end poverty and protect the planet. These goals will form part of the international agenda for sustainable development. The International Women's Health Coalition (IWHC), working with activists from around the world, decided to make sure that reproductive rights were part of that agenda. "We had to fight so much,"

Unsafe abortion today is largely a phenomenon that affects women in **developing countries**. In developed countries, it affects the poorest and most marginalized. So there is a real question of justice, a question of inequality. **Women in poor countries face great danger when they want to terminate a pregnancy.**

—Françoise Girard, IWHC

Since 1998 the Center for Reproductive Rights has produced the World's Abortion Laws map to show the legal status of abortion around the world. The map is regularly updated and interactive: you can access it online at worldabortionlaws.com.

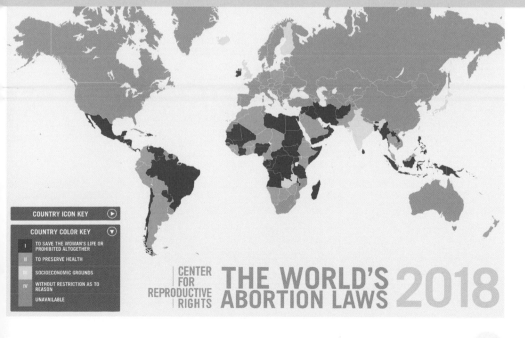

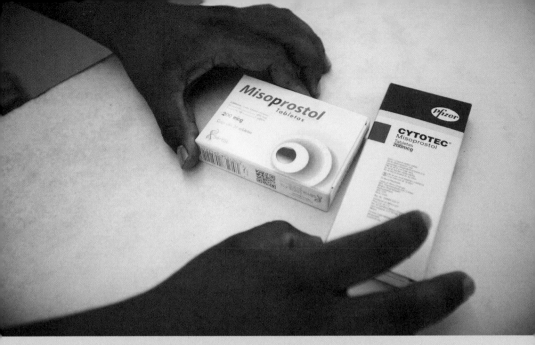

Generic misoprostal and a branded version of the same drug, sold as Cytotec, available for sale at a pharmacy in Mexico. Misoprostal is used to treat stomach ulcers but can also be used to induce abortion.

Françoise Girard, president of IWHC, says. "But 47,000 women are dying every year. So we fought, and we got it in there."

Although the specific challenges are different in different countries, the needs are clear. People need accurate information about their bodies and their reproductive health. They need effective and affordable contraception to prevent unwanted pregnancies. And they need access to safe, legal abortion. Around the world, feminist activists are working hard to achieve all of these goals.

ABORTION PILLS

When we talk about global issues and access to abortion, medical (or medication) abortion is an important part of that conversation. Because pills can be taken by anyone, wherever they are, medical abortion has the potential to make abortion accessible to those who cannot get to abortion clinics. This includes people who live in remote areas and those who live in countries where abortion is illegal or highly restricted.

Mifepristone and misoprostol are now included on the World Health Organization's list of essential medicines. In many countries where abortion is illegal, local activists are working hard to raise awareness of abortion pills and let women know how to get them—sometimes at local pharmacies, where they are sold to treat various other conditions, and sometimes by ordering them online from a safe, reliable source.

GLOBAL IMPACT OF US POLICY

The Trump–Pence administration is having a devastating impact on women's lives and health, not just in the United States, but around the world. One of Donald Trump's first acts as president was to sign an executive order reinstating the "global gag rule." This policy says that **nongovernmental organizations** (NGOs) overseas who receive funding from the US government cannot provide abortion services, counsel patients about abortion, refer them to abortion services or advocate for changes to abortion laws in their countries. Also known as the Mexico City policy, this anti-choice policy has existed under previous Republican administrations going back to 1984. Democratic presidents cancel it, and Republican presidents bring it right back. But Donald Trump didn't just reinstate it—he expanded it, and international health experts say the consequences of that decision could be deadly.

Previous versions of the policy applied only to family-planning agencies—that is, agencies that provide information and access to contraception, enabling people to decide if and when they will have children. The amount of affected funding

While the Hyde Amendment makes _Roe_ an empty promise for poor people in the U.S., the Mexico City Policy demeans it abroad.

You might think that the U.S. government would want to encourage the international provision of a right it supposedly guarantees to its own citizens. But the Mexico City Policy does exactly the opposite.

This policy, also known as the Global Gag Rule, has existed under every Republican president since Reagan.

Under the current rule, the U.S. will not give **any** international health funds* to NGOs that "perform or actively promote abortion as a method of family planning in other nations."

*Past versions applied only to international family planning funds.

came to about $600 million a year. But in developing countries around the world, many organizations that provide a wide range of other health-care services also receive US funding. The United States provides about $9 *billion* in global health assistance every year. In addition to family planning and reproductive health programs, this money funds children's health and nutrition programs, programs to prevent and treat HIV/AIDS, malaria, tuberculosis and other infectious diseases, and even programs that work to ensure drinking water is safe. Under Trump's expanded gag rule, all of these programs are now affected.

Some clinics will close because they are no longer able to get funding. Others will be forced to accept the gag rule, sacrificing their work for safe abortions in order to continue providing other essential services. This means there will be many more unintended pregnancies and many more unsafe abortions. Between 2001 and 2008, the last period when the gag rule was in effect, the number of abortions more than doubled in the African countries most affected by the policy.

SPEAKING OUT

The Mexico City policy is a phenomenally flawed policy. It makes no sense. It's championed by individuals that don't believe in a woman's right to choose and want to reduce access to abortion services. But instead what it does is drive up demand for abortion services because it takes away the ability of women to prevent unintended pregnancy.

—Sarah Shaw, Marie Stopes International

Under the new global gag rule, the most marginalized women and girls will have even less ability to access information and make choices about their own bodies, health and lives. Because of this policy—which is a direct result of the lobbying by the American anti-choice movement—thousands of women and girls around the world will die every year.

REFUSING THE GAG: A MATTER OF PRINCIPLES AND VALUES

Seventeen years ago Fadekemi (Kemi) Akinfaderin-Agarau was a junior at Columbia University in New York City, studying the HIV epidemic. She became curious about the impact it was having in Nigeria, the country of her birth, and decided to return to find out. She also wanted to learn about young people's access to sex education. She had planned to stay in Nigeria for two years, but after working with hundreds of teenagers only a few years younger than herself, she discovered a passion for the work.

I volunteered in a refugee health center in the early 2000s, during a time when the global gag order was in place. We couldn't do abortions... so women had no choice but to try to self-abort. And they would come in, bleeding and injured. I learned—immediately, urgently—that **you can't ban abortion. You can only ban safe abortion**.

–Dr. Adrian Eoin Edgar, Clinic 554, Canada

"I made a lot of friends, and I saw how important this work was, how big the gap was, how the system wasn't set up for sex education. It gave me this resolve that this was what I needed to do. So I gave up the idea of doing medical school. I went back to Columbia and did a two-year degree in public health. Immediately when I was done, I couldn't wait to get back on the plane."

Kemi and a friend started an organization called Education as a Vaccine Against AIDS, but its scope soon expanded to include providing information about sexual and reproductive health, teen pregnancy and safe abortion. So they changed the name to Education as a Vaccine (EVA). Kemi and her friend started to train and support others to provide the information they had been offering, while they began to focus on policy and advocacy in hopes of having a larger impact.

They also embraced the power of technology, starting the My Question service. "Young people can phone a free hotline and speak to a counselor in our office—we have five, speaking different Nigerian languages—or they can ask questions by text message or email," Kemi explains. They've created mobile apps to teach teens about sexual health and help them access services. They advocate for guidelines to ensure that young people can access contraception. And they provide information to teens facing unwanted pregnancy, helping them avoid the complications of unsafe abortions, which are one of the leading causes of maternal death in the country.

Demonstrators in the US protest Trump's global gag order on International Women's Day in March 2017. About two million people around the world took to the streets in an International Women's Strike to show global solidarity and protest continued inequality and violence against women.

A counselor at EVA (Education As Vaccine) answers phone calls, responds to questions and provides information about seual and reproductive health to young people all over Nigeria.

In 2016 EVA had an opportunity to partner with a US organization. "It was a huge amount of money—many millions of dollars— and it was the first time we had been written into a proposal. It would have given us more influence and power; it would have paid more salaries and overhead; we could have expanded our services and reached more young people with our phone line, our community work, our work to help people access HIV services and treatment."

But then Trump signed the expanded version of the global gag rule. Kemi knew that if EVA accepted money from the United States, they could no longer talk to pregnant girls and women about their options. If a teenager called them asking questions about abortion, they would have to say, "We can't talk to you about that." Not only would they be unable to help girls directly, but they also would no longer be able to lobby legislators in Nigeria regarding reproductive health issues, or support other groups working for improved access to safe abortion. In order to continue their life-saving work, they would have to refuse all international funding from the United States.

"We had to make a conscious decision, and it was a very difficult decision to make," Kemi says. "But it was a matter of principles and values. We are an organization that believes in rights." So EVA pulled out of the proposal. They refused to be gagged.

ABORTION IN NOLLYWOOD

Nigeria has a booming movie industry that is sometimes known as Nollywood—in fact, Nollywood is the world's second-largest movie industry, ahead of America's Hollywood and right behind India's Bollywood. Most of the movies playing across Africa are Nollywood films. Unfortunately, if a woman has an abortion in one of these films, she is portrayed as a bad, immoral person—and she usually dies or is horribly injured and unable to have children in the future. Abortion is presented as very dangerous—and this affects the beliefs of many people all over Africa.

"The movie industry has a huge role to play in terms of shifting public opinion and these misconceptions and blatant lies about abortion," says Fadekemi Akinfaderin-Agarau. "If people realize that abortion is actually safe, they are more likely to support **liberalization** of laws. But they see abortion as dangerous, so they say, 'Why would we push for something that kills people?'"

Actors and crew on a Nollywood film set. Nollywood produces over 1,500 movies a year—far more than America's Hollywood.

Three weeks after Savita's death, more than ten thousand people took part in a rally on the streets of Dublin. Savita's father spoke out publicly and called on Ireland's government to change the law on abortion.

FIGHTING FOR ABORTION RIGHTS IN IRELAND

In 1983 Ireland added an Eighth Amendment to its constitution. This amendment said that the fetus had a right to life equal to that of its mother and that Irish laws must defend that right. During the decades that followed, abortion remained banned— and every year thousands of Irish residents traveled abroad to have abortions. The majority of them went to England. In 2016, 3,265 patients gave Irish addresses at abortion services in the UK. Groups such as the Abortion Support Network did what they could to help. Run mostly by volunteers and supported by private donations, the Abortion Support Network provided information, financial assistance and accommodation to people from Ireland who needed to travel to England to get abortions.

In 2012 Savita Halappanavar's death made national headlines. Savita, a thirty-one-year-old dentist, was seventeen weeks pregnant when she was admitted to hospital and found to be miscarrying.

She was in severe pain and wanted the doctors to do an abortion, but because there was still a fetal heartbeat, this was not allowed under Irish law. Savita developed *sepsis*, a life-threatening complication, and died in hospital. Experts testified that she could have lived if she had been given an abortion as she requested. Savita's death led to widespread outrage and increased support for changing the abortion laws in Ireland. The campaign for legal abortion in Ireland was referred to as the campaign to "repeal the 8th."

When the Eighth Amendment was introduced, after significant lobbying by Catholic groups, about 70 percent of voters supported it. But Irish society has changed a lot since the early eighties. The influence of the Catholic Church has lessened,

SPEAKING OUT

It is impossible to be a young person in today's Irish society and not know something about the 8th. **You can't walk through the city center without seeing Repeal sprayed on walls or pro-choice stickers on lampposts.**

—Megan Brady, activist, co-founder of School Students for Choice

Activists in Dublin, Ireland, campaign for the repeal of the Eighth Amendment after the death of Savita Halappanavar.

and young people in particular are leading the way in making social change. In 2015 they voted overwhelmingly in favor of marriage equality. The Abortion Rights Campaign (ARC) in the Republic of Ireland has grown rapidly—3,000 people attended the March for Choice in 2012. In 2016 more than 20,000 showed up.

Pressure was building, and the government responded. On May 25, 2018, Ireland held a *referendum*, and people voted on whether to repeal the Eighth Amendment. The result was a decisive victory for abortion rights, with two thirds voting *yes* to repeal. Irish citizens from around the world flew home to vote. Twenty-three-year-old Ause Abdelhaq-Braike made the

Teenagers in Ireland—including many who are too young to vote—have played an important role in the fight for abortion rights.

Although this photo became the iconic image of the HomeToVote movement, it was actually taken two years before the referendum, at a protest in front of the Irish embassy in London, UK. Protesters brought suitcases to symbolize the thousands of people who had to travel from Ireland to England to get abortions.

twelve-hour trip from Nairobi, Kenya. "I hope history remembers us as the generation that finally drew a line in the sand," he said. "We finally did away with the religious guilt and shame that has been hanging over our country for centuries."

This vote to repeal the Eighth Amendment clears the way for the government to make a new law that will allow first-trimester abortions to be performed in the country. It is a huge victory for those who have fought for reproductive rights in Ireland—and it will likely send ripples around the globe. "I think we lit a beacon of hope for countries all over the world where people are working towards similar change," said Grainne Griffin of the Together for Yes campaign.

In neighboring Northern Ireland, the only part of the United Kingdom where abortion is still criminalized, advocates are vowing that they will not be left behind. In Poland, Natalia Broniarczyk of Warsaw's Abortion Dream Team said, "Social

Thousands of YES voters across Ireland took to the streets to celebrate their landslide victory in the referendum on repealing the Eighth Amendment.

movements around women's rights in Poland will take some hope from it." And for Catholic countries such as Argentina, the Irish referendum is a sign that change is possible.

The day after the referendum, Leo Varadkar, Taoiseach (prime minister) of the Republic of Ireland, called the vote the culmination of a quiet revolution. "No more doctors telling their patients there is nothing that can be done for them in their own country," he said. "No more lonely journeys across the Irish Sea. No more stigma. The veil of secrecy is lifted. No more isolation. The burden of shame is gone."

Savita Halappanavar's father, Andanappa Yalagi, also shared his reaction. "We've got justice for Savita, and what happened to her will not happen to any other family now," he said.

YOUNG ACTIVISTS:
Ireland

Meet three of the young activists who have been a part of the fight for choice in Dublin, Ireland: Megan Brady (center) and her friends Niamh Scully (right) and Jodie Doyle (left). They're high school students and members and co-founders of a group called School Students for Choice.

When Megan was thirteen, she began learning about the Eighth Amendment and went with friends to a pro-choice march. A couple of years later she became more involved, joining the socialist feminist group ROSA (for Reproductive rights, against Oppression, Sexism & Austerity). Megan's work with ROSA inspired her and her friends to set up School Students for Choice, a group that held student protest rallies and more informal activities, such as pro-choice picnics in the park, to help students learn about the movement to repeal the Eighth Amendment.

Like Megan, Jodie also became involved by attending ROSA meetings, but she adds, "I think my first proper 'involvement' was just buying a badge [button]...and I think, especially for younger activists, something that small is still a really important step to make because it just shows they're willing to be open and proud about their opinion!"

Along with other members of School Students for Choice, the three activists spoke publicly at events, attended rallies and protests, organized petitions and postcard campaigns and put on an event called "A Night for Repeal," which featured poets and musicians performing pieces about feminism and reproductive rights. Another form of activism

this group has engaged in is conversation—online and in person—talking to people and explaining why they support abortion rights.

"I personally believe the only way to move forward is for us all to listen to other people, no matter how hard their opinion may be to hear," Niamh says. "We can never convince anti-choice people of the importance of full bodily autonomy without truly understanding why they are so against it in the first place."

They also see a role for louder, more visible forms of protest. "Sometimes shouting is what needs to be done to be heard and listened to," Niamh says.

Jodie agrees, adding, "Just get out and do something and don't be afraid—be as loud as you possibly can!"

The historic referendum of May 25, 2018, was the opportunity the three activists had been working toward for years. "The day of the vote, I was frantically reaching out to so many people, making sure they made it to the polls," Megan says. "I cannot put into words how I felt when I saw the exit poll. I was in shock. The next day I felt proud of Ireland and of all the work we had done to secure this victory. That landslide YES vote has proven that the people of Ireland will no longer support the backwards ideas of the Catholic Church that have had an iron grip on our country for too long. This victory has given me hope that the people of Ireland will continue to fight to make our home the progressive, compassionate place I know it can be."

Megan, Niamh and Jodie hope that new legislation will soon be put in place to ensure that abortion is legal and accessible to all who need it. But all three activists are aware that some obstacles remain: the stigma that surrounds abortion, the power of the Church and the possibility that even after the Eighth is repealed, the predominantly Catholic hospitals might be reluctant to provide abortions. "I still believe that there will be some fierce obstacles ahead, but I do get some comfort from the decisive victory," Megan says. "The huge amount of people that fought for repeal will not just disappear; I have faith that we will press on...This fight is far from over, and I think all those amazing repealers are ready to keep going on."

A protester in Krakow, Poland, taking part in the October 2016 nationwide women's strike against a proposed total ban on abortion in Poland.

WOMEN'S STRIKE IN POLAND

Abortion was legal in Poland until 1993, when the Catholic Church succeeded in pushing its anti-contraception, anti-abortion agenda into the political mainstream. Before long the country had some of the most restrictive abortion laws in Europe. In 2016 the government began considering a new law—a total ban on abortion that would include jail time for anyone who had an abortion and any doctors who assisted them.

Doctors warned that this law would make it dangerous for them to do standard prenatal tests, such as **amniocentesis**, which carry a small risk of causing miscarriage. Women who developed preeclampsia—a condition that can occur late in pregnancy, causing dangerously high blood pressure—would have to be left to die, along with their fetuses. A doctor who followed the standard lifesaving protocol of delivering the baby by cesarean section would risk jail time if the premature infant did not survive.

Women in Poland decided to go on strike in protest. About 30,000 women marched through the streets of the capital city, Warsaw, dressed in black—a symbol of mourning for their loss of reproductive rights. Inspired by a women's strike in Iceland in 1975, they refused to go to work or to school. In over sixty cities across Poland women held protests, and throughout Europe supporters organized demonstrations to show support and solidarity.

And the protests worked. Just three days after the strike, the government backed away from the proposed abortion ban. Polls showed that the protests had also shifted public opinion on the issue—not only was there strong opposition to the proposed ban, but there was also increased support for relaxing the existing abortion law. Aleksandra Włodarczyk, one of the women who took

Protesters in Wroclaw, Poland, demonstrating against a proposed total ban on abortion, as part of a nationwide women's strike.

part in the protests, said, "In previous anti-government protests, it was our parents' generation on the streets. But with this, they have managed to mobilize the young, and we are very angry."

WOMEN ON WAVES

Although abortion is criminalized in many countries, there is one place where no government can make it illegal: in international waters. International waters begin 12 nautical miles (22.2 kilometers/13.8 miles) from the shore of a country's coastline. When a ship is in international waters, the laws of its own country apply. So on Rebecca Gomperts's Dutch boat, abortion is legal.

Rebecca is the founder and director of Women on Waves. A physician, artist, writer and women's rights activist from the Netherlands, she has devoted her career to advocating for abortion

"It all started when I was working at Greenpeace as the ship's doctor in countries where abortion was illegal. I'd seen a lot of women brought in severely bleeding or in shock because of illegal abortions. I realized that there is a connection between the law and the fact that women are dying. **I could not observe that and just let it happen."**

—Rebecca Gomperts, founder and director of Women on Waves, in the documentary film *Vessel*

In 2004 Women on Waves chartered the ship Borndiep and sailed it to Portugal, where it was declared a security threat nd forbidden to enter national waters.

rights and helping women around the world get safe abortions. Women on Waves sails to countries with restrictive abortion laws. So far they have visited Ireland, Poland, Portugal, Spain, Morocco, Mexico and Guatemala. Working with local organizations, the group invites women who want to end their pregnancies to board the ship. The ship then moves offshore into international waters, where the women can take the abortion pill.

In addition to directly helping the women who are able to board the ship, these campaigns help in other ways. Sailing an abortion ship into the harbor of a country where abortion is illegal (and often taboo) generates a huge amount of publicity. The publicity helps break down the stigma about abortion, normalizes it as a procedure that is safe and common, and promotes conversation about the topic. Sometimes this leads to dramatic change. What happened in Portugal illustrates the power of this strategy.

Fifteen years ago many Portuguese women were suffering because of the restrictive abortion laws. Every year more than 20,000 illegal abortions were performed, and approximately

5,000 women were hospitalized with complications. Occasionally women died. Many women had been prosecuted for having illegal abortions. In August 2004, Women on Waves, at the invitation of local organizations, sailed to Portugal…and Portugal forbade the ship from entering its national waters. The Portuguese minister of defense claimed it posed a severe threat to national security and sent two warships to monitor the boat as it waited in international waters.

An abortion drone flying abortion pills from the Republic of Ireland to Northern Ireland. After the drone landed, two women took the pills.

Unable to enter the harbor, Women on Waves found another way to help. One of the abortion drugs, misoprostol, was available in pharmacies in Portugal because it is used to prevent stomach ulcers and to treat arthritis. Rebecca Gomperts went on Portuguese television and explained how women could get misoprostol and use it to end an unwanted pregnancy. She said that Women on Waves would publish a protocol on its website for how to use misoprostol safely. Hundreds of women contacted the organization to request it. The misoprostol page remains their most visited web page.

Over the weeks that the abortion ship sat offshore, Women on Waves received many hours of television coverage. More than 700 newspaper articles were published in Portugal alone, and the subject of abortion was forced onto the national agenda. In September 2004 the ship and its crew returned to the Netherlands, but a poll conducted later that month found that almost 80 percent of the Portuguese people supported a new referendum on abortion law, and 60 percent believed abortion should be decriminalized. The outpouring of support was too powerful to ignore.

Over 130 people participated in a flash mob in Yogyakarta, Indonesia. The event publicized the phone number of a safe-abortion hotline that gives people information on how to get and use abortion pills to end a pregnancy safely.

In 2007 a referendum showed that a majority favored legal abortion, and the government changed the law, making it legal for women to get abortions in the first ten weeks of pregnancy.

A 2015 Women on Waves campaign involved not a boat but a drone, which carried abortion pills over an international border. The drone flew from Germany and crossed the Oder River to land in Słubice, Poland. Two Polish women swallowed the abortion pills. In 2016 the abortion drone flew from the Republic of Ireland into Northern Ireland as an act of solidarity between women in both countries. Women on Waves has also used a remote-controlled speedboat to send more pills to Irish women. In May 2018, just days after Ireland's referendum, they used an abortion robot operated from Amsterdam to deliver pills in Belfast, Northern Ireland.

Women on Waves has also supported the launch of safe-abortion hotlines, working with local activists and women's groups in many countries, including Chile, Peru, Venezuela, Argentina,

Pakistan, Indonesia, Kenya, Thailand, Poland and Morocco. The hotlines are staffed by volunteers who can tell women how to get and use misoprostol to end their pregnancies.

WOMEN ON WEB

Women on Web is an international collective that answers questions and provides information about abortion. The group also helps women get contraceptives and abortions. It provides abortion pills to women all over the world—in European countries such as Poland and Ireland, as well as in many countries in South America, the Middle East, Africa and Asia.

Women on Web is a sister organization to Women on Waves. Ellen Wiebe, a Canadian abortion provider who sits on the board of directors for Women on Web, says, "In all the media interviews, they [Women on Waves] say that women can find them on Women on Web—and then we get thousands of women contacting us and accessing abortions that way."

The organization's model is simple and effective. Women who live in countries where they cannot access abortion safely and legally are referred to a doctor for an online consultation. Following the consultation—a series of questions to be answered online, in the woman's own language—Women on Web will arrange for abortion pills to be delivered to them. For women who are less than ten weeks pregnant, these abortion pills are a safe and effective method of ending a pregnancy.

Women who access abortion pills through Women on Web are asked to make a donation if they can, but those who are unable to pay will not be turned away. Donations from women who can afford to pay for their abortion pills help cover the costs of pills for those living in poverty.

Women on Waves offers Safe Abortion stickers that provide information on getting and using abortion pills to end a pregnancy safely. The stickers are available in more than a dozen languages and can be printed from the website and pasted in public places.

The website also fights stigma by providing a place for women to share the stories of their abortions. These stories, from all over the world, provide a glimpse into the lives and choices of women dealing with unwanted pregnancies.

Women on Web stickers are available in many languages and can be printed out and stuck in public places to let women know how they can access medical advice and get abortion pills online.

Another nonprofit organization, Women Help Women, works on a similar model, providing abortion pills and contraceptives to women around the world. It and Women on Web offer hope and help to thousands of women every year, preventing many unsafe abortions and protecting the lives and future health of many girls and women.

Unfortunately, there are also dozens of scams—websites that prey on desperate women. These sites promise to send abortion pills but just take people's money and send pills that are ineffective and possibly dangerous. Sometimes they send nothing at all.

YOUNG ACTIVISTS:
Turkey

Hazal Atay is a young activist from Turkey. She is a member of an international organization of young people called the Youth Coalition for Sexual and Reproductive Rights (YCSRR). Abortion is legal in Turkey, but in 2012 the prime minister and other government officials spoke out against it. Rumors circulated that a new anti-abortion law would be introduced. Women's groups across the country organized protests, and although the existing law wasn't changed, abortion stigma increased, public hospitals began turning patients away and abortion services became less accessible. Hazal says, "The government's attack on abortion rights shook us and taught us that we should continue to fight for our rights even if they were already gained."

Hazal heard about the Women on Waves campaign in Morocco. Soon she had joined Women on Web as a new team member, and she worked to establish help desks for women in the Middle East and North Africa. "I was truly inspired with women's determination to take an ownership of their future despite the restrictive laws of their countries," Hazal says.

The current political situation in Turkey is difficult, and many human rights advocates have been arrested, imprisoned or threatened. Since the attempted coup in 2016, some feminist organizations, journals and newspapers have shut down. Numerous websites are also banned—among them, Women on Web.

"Despite this situation," Hazal says, "I am still hopeful for the future. I am hopeful that we had some good laws in the past, and I am hopeful that we have amazing people who are determined to fight back."

For health, equality, justice, choice...

REPEAL THE 8TH!

A new leadership program called Youth Testify is specifically for young people who have had abortions and want to share their stories.

BEHIND THE SCENES: WORKING FOR SOCIAL CHANGE

Dramatic legal victories tend to make headlines around the world. But in many countries, governments are unwilling to consider decriminalizing abortion or even engage in conversations about abortion rights. In those places, a great deal of work is going on behind the scenes. Activists all over the world are working hard to reduce stigma and overcome the taboos that make many people reluctant to talk about abortion. They are creating space for conversations about *sexual and reproductive health and rights (SRHR)*. They are encouraging feminist organizations, women's groups and health networks to put this topic on their agendas. They are starting support groups to help women facing unwanted pregnancies, and running education campaigns and hotlines to let women know about abortion pills. In the short term, their work helps many desperate women—and saves lives. And in the longer term, it helps shift attitudes and build national movements that can eventually lead to campaigns for legal abortion.

YOUNG ACTIVISTS:
Madagascar

Lova Andrianina Randrianasolo is a sexual and reproductive health and rights (SRHR) advocate in Madagascar, a large island nation off the southeast coast of Africa. "My country is a very traditional one," Lova explains. "Sex is a taboo [subject] in my country...Not so many adolescents in Madagascar can talk about sex and have access to information about it."

But as a young teenager, Lova was curious. She went to the library with a friend. "We read books about it, we learned alone about everything: what is sexual identity, what is sexual intercourse...but all the basic information we didn't know about contraceptive, abortion, etc." As Lova learned more about issues of youth and sexuality, she became interested in the concept of sexual and reproductive health and rights—human rights applied to the areas of sexuality and reproduction. "At the age of seventeen I was convinced that adolescents and young people in Madagascar need to have support," Lova says. "I joined my cousin and we co-founded a youth-led organization that works to help young people in Madagascar access information, to know about their rights."

Lova is now 24, and the organization she founded, Youth First, has become one of the most influential youth-led organizations in the country. Lova works as a project manager and has developed a leadership program to empower Malagasy girls and young women. She is passionate about human rights and believes in the importance of equality for all. "When I was young I had the chance to get knowledge... but not so many young people have the same opportunity in Madagascar. Reproductive rights are important because

young people are vulnerable. We need to give them good education including SRHR information so that they can take decisions for their body," Lova says.

Sexual education is not part of high-school programs in Madagascar, so teens tend to get their information from friends. Contraception is not easily accessible for young people, so they often face unwanted pregnancies. Some feel they have no choice but to get married. Others find support from international organizations that provide information and send abortion pills.

Lova advocates for comprehensive sex education. "The more information young people get, the more they are autonomous to take decisions." She is less optimistic about the future of abortion rights in her country. "Abortion is illegal and will stay illegal for the long term," she says. "I stay hopeful, but I am convinced that it will take longer until this issue will change."

YOUNG ACTIVISTS:
Venezuela

Abortion is highly restricted or banned in most Latin American and Caribbean countries. At least 10 percent of all maternal deaths in the region are due to unsafe abortions. In Venezuela, where women can go to jail for ending a pregnancy, unsafe abortion is the second-biggest killer of young women.

Isabel Pérez Witzke is a young Venezuelan SRHR activist who is working for change. "I decided that I wanted to do something for people who needed abortions because I felt that the topic completely challenges what I was taught about womanhood, what it signifies to the world: to be a woman is to be a mother. And to have an abortion is to break that imposed life purpose."

In 2014 Isabel joined a grassroots feminist organization called Red de Información por el Aborto Seguro (RIAS), or Information Network for Safe Abortion. RIAS runs a twenty-four-hour helpline that provides safe-abortion information to callers. It also works to destigmatize abortion and build public support for abortion rights. Isabel helped staff the safe-abortion helpline. She says, "Being part of RIAS gave me the opportunity to understand what a lot of women felt about themselves because of the weight of abortion stigma. People usually think that they are completely impulsive when the reality is that this is one of the most responsible decisions they are taking. It takes time, it takes courage and is taken with eyes wide open."

After telling callers how to use abortion pills, Isabel usually asked them if they would be willing to answer a few survey questions. "The final question was about their opinion on abortion legislation, if they consider that abortion should be legal or no. It was interesting that most of them impulsively answered

a huge *no*, but after a pause several of them reconsidered...
The call was not only a space for providing information but
to *talk*, to listen and to analyze this topic...And the space was
profoundly appreciated because women always said how
grateful they were with us because we heard them, we listened."

After her work with RIAS, Isabel interned with a local
organization supporting young mothers and providing sexuality
education. She then went on to work with Asociación Civil de
Planificación Familiar (PLAFAM), or the Civil Association of
Family Planning. She promotes youth participation in SRHR and
supports peer education. She also helps young people access
services that are based on a **harm reduction model**—a model of
care built on supporting people's rights to make their own choices.

"There are important things being done even though there
have been no significant changes at a legislative level," Isabel
says. "We need to understand that we all are valuable, we all
have something to say, and we all need safe spaces where our
voice is valid. When we don't have that space we need to fight
for it; we need to construct it. And the only way to construct
them is when we fight together. So, listen, connect and be part
of change!"

BE ORGANIZED and BE MANY

— HAZAL ATAY

#safeabortion

#Prochoice

#reproductivefreedom

#IstandwithPlannedParenth

#1in3speaks

#shoutyourabortion

#womensrighttochoose

#abortthestig

#abortolibre

#celebrateabortionprovid

#humanrights

CHAPTER FIVE

THE WAY FORWARD: STORIES FROM THE FRONT LINES

A bortion has been a safe, legal and common procedure in Canada and the United States for many years now, but there is still a lot of work to be done. Silence and stigma continue to surround the subject, making it difficult for people to talk about their experiences. And although abortion is legal, it is not always accessible. Many people, especially young people and those who are marginalized, face barriers in accessing care. Anti-choice politicians and lobby groups are trying to undermine the gains that have been made. But people who are committed to reproductive rights are working hard, on many fronts, to end abortion stigma and create a world in which abortion is legal, safe and accessible to all. In this chapter you will read some of their stories.

MOVING FROM CHOICE TO REPRODUCTIVE JUSTICE

Throughout the 1960s, '70s and '80s, feminists organized around the concept of choice. Today people still talk about the pro-choice movement or the right to choose. But in the 1990s, women of color

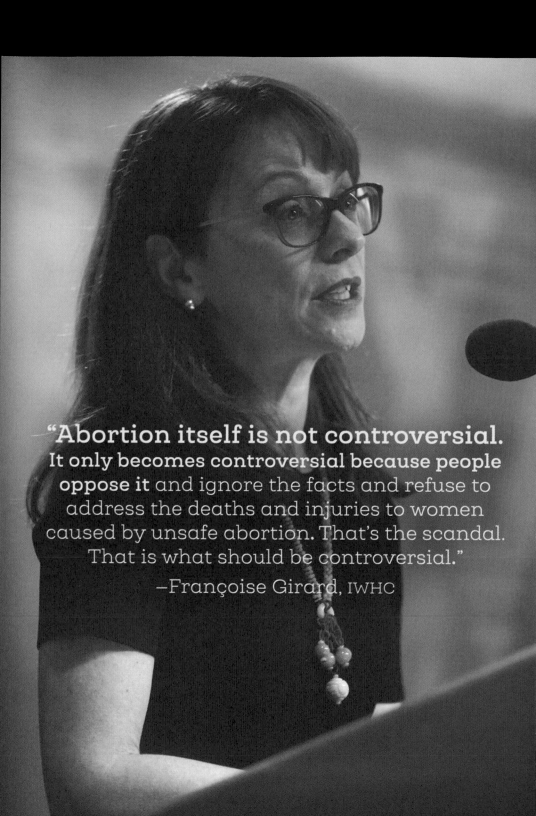

"Abortion itself is not controversial. It only becomes controversial because people oppose it and ignore the facts and refuse to address the deaths and injuries to women caused by unsafe abortion. That's the scandal. That is what should be controversial."
—Françoise Girard, IWHC

in the United States began speaking out together, pointing out the limitations of the language and the concept of choice. For one thing, *choice* focused almost entirely on a woman's legal right to prevent pregnancy and get an abortion. But throughout history, women of color also had to fight for their right to have and raise their children in safe communities. They agreed that abortion and contraception needed to be legal and safe, but argued that this in itself was not sufficient and did not address the needs of the most vulnerable. If abortion is legal but someone can't afford to travel hundreds of miles to get to a clinic, is that truly a choice? If a woman has to have an abortion because she can't afford contraception and can't afford to raise a child, is that truly a choice?

Based in Atlanta, GA, the SisterSong Women of Color Reproductive Justice Collective has been a leader in promoting reproductive justice since it was founded in the late 1990s.

In 1994 a group of Black women in Chicago came together to discuss a new national movement that would focus on the needs of the most marginalized people and communities. They named their group Women of African Descent for Reproductive Justice—giving birth to a phrase that would go on to transform the politics of reproductive rights.

One organization that has played a leading role in developing and promoting a theory of **reproductive justice** is SisterSong. Based in Atlanta and founded in 1997 by Loretta Ross, Luz Rodriguez and others, SisterSong has developed a framework that places the idea of reproductive rights in a context of social justice.

Reproductive justice demands that people have the right to have a child, the right *not* to have a child and the right to parent children in safe and healthy environments. Like the pro-choice

The language of choice doesn't take into account our lived experience. It doesn't take into account the societal factors that affect us and limit our options. If you can't afford an abortion, you don't have a choice. If you can't afford the time off work, or can't travel the distance to get to a clinic, you don't have a choice. Or if saving up the money takes too long, the choice is taken away from you. If you can't afford to have another child, you don't have a choice. The language of choice ignores the social realities, the sets of circumstances, within which people make decisions. **For many people, there is no choice.**

–Renee Bracey Sherman, reproductive justice activist, writer and expert on abortion storytelling

movement, reproductive justice demands that abortion be safe, legal and accessible—but it doesn't stop there. For full reproductive justice to be achieved, *all* people, including the most marginalized, need to be able to access not just abortion services but also sex education, birth control, health care, protection from violence, support for raising children and safe housing in which to raise them.

Reproductive justice suggests that we can't look at the issue of abortion rights without understanding the larger context of people's lives or without addressing the multiple forms of oppression people face. This framework is influencing how people think about, talk about and advocate for abortion.

WILLIE PARKER

Opposition to abortion is sometimes connected to people's religious beliefs. However, there are also religious groups that support reproductive rights and access to abortion. As you read in chapter 1, the Clergy Consultation Service helped women access abortions before they became legal. And from that underground network evolved the Religious Coalition for Reproductive Choice (RCRC). It represents a diverse group of organizations, religions and theologies that stand together to work for reproductive health, rights and justice.

Dr. Willie Parker is an abortion provider who is also a passionate writer and speaker. He promotes abortion rights and reproductive rights in his book Life's Work.

Today, some abortion providers choose to do this work not *despite* their religious beliefs but *because* of them. One such person is RCRC leader Dr. Willie Parker.

Willie Parker grew up in a segregated neighborhood in Birmingham, Alabama. He was raised in a Black Christian church community in which, he recalls, "an unplanned pregnancy was reason enough for a public shaming, or even expulsion from church ministry." For the first half of his medical career he refused to perform abortions. But as time went on, and as he spoke with patients who were seeking abortions, he began to feel uncomfortable with his inaction. "I believed in a woman's right to choose," he recalls. "But I was complicit with anti-abortion forces in that I did not place myself on the front lines."

Willie Parker was deeply influenced by his beliefs and values as a Christian, and by the powerful words of Dr. Martin Luther King Jr.—some of which were penned in a jail cell less than ten miles from where Willie Parker grew up: *Injustice anywhere is a threat to justice everywhere.* And in 2002, while living in Hawaii, Dr. Parker was watching injustice unfold. The administrator of the clinic where he worked had decided that they would no longer offer abortion services. This would mean that only those who could afford private physicians would be able to access abortions. Dr. Parker was deeply concerned about the suffering this would cause the poor women the clinic was supposed to serve. "To me, it wasn't acceptable to deny them a safe and legal procedure. It wasn't right."

Dr. Willie Parker is chair of the board of Physicians for Reproductive Health and part of the leadership of the Religious Coalition for Reproductive Choice.

He went home that day angry and frustrated. That evening he turned to Dr. King for comfort and inspiration, and listened to an audiotape of "I've Been to the Mountaintop," Dr. King's final speech. The story of the Good Samaritan, and Dr. King's musings about that story, hit him hard. "Like a punch, all at once, in my spiritual gut...The earth spun, and the question turned on its head. It became not *Is it right for me, as a Christian, to perform abortions?* but rather *Is it right for me, as a Christian, to refuse to do them?*" The next day he told his colleagues that he wanted to learn how to do abortions, and soon after he was training full time in abortion care. Since that time he has dedicated himself to this work, giving up his private practice to provide abortions in Mississippi, Alabama and Georgia.

"As an African American man descended from slaves and raised in the South, it is too easy for me to imagine what it's like to have no control over your body, your destiny, your life," he says. "I believe that as an abortion provider I am doing God's work. Performing abortions, and speaking out on behalf of the women who want abortions, is my calling. It is my life's work."

IMPROVING ACCESS FOR ALL: DIVERSITY AND ABORTION SERVICES

While anyone who can become pregnant may find themselves facing an unwanted pregnancy, some groups have difficulty accessing services. Although abortion is legal across Canada and the United States, people in remote communities, in rural areas and in states and provinces with more restrictions have less access. Low-income people, transgender people, people with disabilities, immigrants, refugees and undocumented people also face additional barriers.

REMOTE COMMUNITIES AND THE PROMISE OF TELEMEDICINE

Because Canada is so large and the population so spread out, access to medical services, including abortion, is a problem for many remote communities. One possible strategy to improve access in these communities is to provide medical abortions through telemedicine.

In 1993 Ellen Wiebe became the first doctor in Canada to do a medical abortion. She is also a pioneer in the field of abortion telemedicine. "In BC," she says, "we have been able to use telemedicine to provide medical abortion, which improves access to

Ellen Wiebe was the first doctor in Canada to do a medical abortion, and her pioneering clinical trials led to the approval of Mifegymiso.

abortion in small communities. A doctor will see the patient by Skype or FaceTime, the patient can talk to our counselor the same way, and they can get their blood work done in a lab in their own community." Patients still early in their pregnancies can be given abortion pills and have their abortions at home.

But the potential for telemedicine and medical abortion to improve access is still largely unrealized. Canada has been slow to develop its medical abortion program. The abortion drug combination known as RU-486, licensed in France in 1988 and approved for use in the United States in 2000, only recently became widely available for use in Canada, where it is known as Mifegymiso. So far, few doctors are making it available to their patients.

Sandeep Prasad, the executive director of Action Canada for Sexual Health and Rights, an Ottawa-based advocacy organization, says he is not aware of any physicians outside of abortion clinics who are prescribing Mifegymiso. "We really need large numbers of family physicians...to ensure that we are realizing the game-changing potential of Mifegymiso."

Part of the problem is a lack of information about medical abortion. "Do women know it's an option? How would they find out? How do you search for something you haven't ever heard about?" Ellen Wiebe says. But people like her are working hard to raise awareness—and hopefully telemedicine will offer a real alternative to many more people in the not-too-distant future.

TRANSGENDER PEOPLE AND ABORTION

Most people facing unwanted pregnancies are women, but some are not. Many transgender men have uteruses and can become pregnant, and these men face significant barriers to accessing reproductive health care. There are also many people who identify as neither male nor female. This includes people with **non-binary, agender, genderqueer, genderfluid** and other **gender identities**. This population is growing rapidly, and studies suggest that it will continue to grow as today's teens and young adults challenge **binary** ideas about gender.

Trans men and non-binary people who can become pregnant need to be able to access necessary care such as routine screening for cancer, contraception to prevent pregnancy and abortion to end unwanted pregnancies. Trans and non-binary people often experience challenges accessing sexual-health services that support their gender identities and their bodies, and as a result

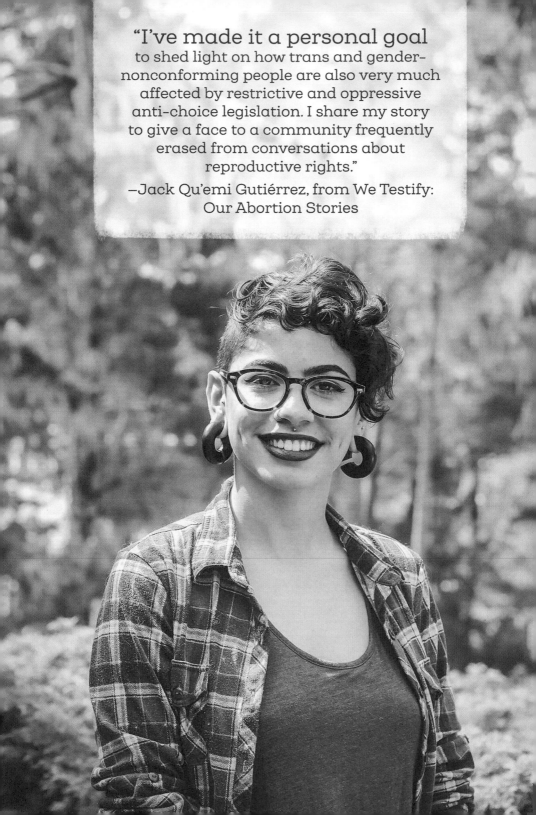

"I've made it a personal goal to shed light on how trans and gender-nonconforming people are also very much affected by restrictive and oppressive anti-choice legislation. I share my story to give a face to a community frequently erased from conversations about reproductive rights."

—Jack Qu'emi Gutiérrez, from We Testify: Our Abortion Stories

some trans people avoid seeking care—or are forced to accept care that fails to support their gender identity.

There are some simple things that medical staff, educators and advocates can do to be more supportive of all people seeking abortions—and contraception and other health care as well. Using **trans-inclusive language** helps ensure that the needs of transgender people are visible. In hospitals and clinics, paperwork often sends a message—so clinic intake and consent forms can refer to *the patient* rather than *the woman*. Doctors and nurses can ask patients what name they prefer to be called and what **pronouns** they use. Education is crucial, as people unfamiliar with these issues often worry about saying the wrong thing. Specific staff training on transgender issues can help create services that are more accessible, appropriate and inclusive.

DISABILITY RIGHTS AND ABORTION

The disability rights community has a complicated relationship with the abortion rights movement. Issues around prenatal screening and selective abortions of fetuses with Down syndrome, spina bifida and other conditions have sparked difficult and often painful debates. And historically people with all kinds of disabilities have been targeted in campaigns of coerced or forced sterilization. They have had to fight for the right to be sexual, to conceive children, to continue pregnancies and to raise their children. But there is also common ground between the two movements. Both disability rights and reproductive rights advocates believe that people should have control over their own bodies and that government should not interfere in people's personal reproductive decisions.

One problem is that in our society, people with disabilities are often not seen as sexual beings, so they may not be given access to sex education and reproductive health care. But they too experience unwanted pregnancies, and they often face even more barriers when they seek abortion services. They may lack suitable transportation to get to doctor's appointments. They may encounter inaccessible medical facilities, clinics that lack the equipment to transfer a patient safely from a wheelchair, or staff unable to interpret sign language. Or they may rely on caregivers who are not supportive of their choices.

We need to ensure that everyone has the resources they need to make the best decisions for themselves and their families, and that everyone can access the information and services they need. This means ensuring that all people have access to comprehensive sex education. It means ensuring that clinics and reproductive health services are accessible. It means ensuring that the lives of people with disabilities are valued and that their voices are heard. And it means that when a prenatal diagnosis reveals a disability, the people involved are given the most accurate and complete information possible, including realistic perspectives from those who live with the disability in question. If people in this situation want an abortion, they need access to supportive abortion services. If they want to carry the pregnancy to term, they need access to appropriate medical, educational and social supports for themselves, their child and their family.

IMMIGRANTS, REFUGEES AND UNDOCUMENTED PEOPLE

Language barriers, financial difficulties and a lack of culturally appropriate services and interpreters can all pose challenges for

Jane Doe supporters gathered near the Washington, DC, courthouse where her case was heard in October 2017. On social media many people demanded #JusticeforJane. (Lauryn Gutierrez © Rewire.News)

immigrants and refugees needing reproductive health care and abortion services. The US government has also directly attacked the rights of undocumented people to get abortions. In the fall of 2017 a seventeen-year-old girl, referred to in the media as Jane Doe, became part of a high-profile legal battle when she was blocked from getting an abortion and prevented from leaving the detention center where she was being held. Federal and state officials argued that because of her immigration status, her right to get an abortion in the United States was not protected. This teenager ultimately succeeded in getting an abortion, but three similar cases have since been confirmed and taken to court by

While the government provides for most of my needs at the shelter, they have not allowed me to leave to get an abortion. Instead, they made me see a doctor that tried to convince me not to abort and to look at sonograms. People I don't even know are trying to make me change my mind. I made my decision and that is between me and God. Through all of this, I have never changed my mind. No one should be shamed for making the right decision for themselves. I would not tell any other girl in my situation what they should do. That decision is hers and hers alone.

—Jane Doe, in a public statement made via her guardian

the American Civil Liberties Union. They are known anonymously as Jane Roe, Jane Poe and Jane Moe. It is likely that there are others also being denied their rights: there are many undocumented pregnant teens in custody in the United States, and the Trump administration seems to be willing to go to great lengths to prevent them from getting abortions.

GRASSROOTS ACTIVISM

Even back before abortion was legalized, people started forming groups and raising money to help people get abortions. Grassroots groups still help people access abortion services today.

ABORTION FUNDS

When the Hyde Amendment banned Medicaid from paying for abortions in the United States, organizations called *abortion funds* started to form because people couldn't afford their abortions. The National Network of Abortion Funds began when some of the individual groups decided that they needed to coordinate and share resources. There are now seventy abortion funds in thirty-eight states, and they respond to more than 100,000 calls each year from people who can't afford their abortions. They've expanded in scope as well, offering not just money but also practical supports—someone to talk to, a place to stay, a ride to a clinic in a strange city.

Shannon Hardy is a social worker in Halifax, NS, who volunteers as an abortion doula—a support person for people who are having abortions. She runs Abortion Support Services Atlantic (formerly Maritime Abortion Support Services).

SUPPORTING ACCESS IN ATLANTIC CANADA

For many years Prince Edward Island had poor access to abortion services. It also had some creative, resourceful and committed activists working to change that. In 2012 Shannon Hardy, a sexual health educator from Halifax, Nova Scotia, was concerned about the fact that residents of Prince Edward Island couldn't get abortions in their own province and were forced to travel several hours to Halifax to end a pregnancy. She thought there needed to be some kind of organization to assist them, so she decided to start one. Along with other organizers, she founded the Maritime Abortion Support Services (MASS). Volunteers in PEI drove people to the bridge between PEI and New Brunswick, and volunteers from Halifax, Nova Scotia, picked them up, drove them to the hospital and provided safe, free places for them to stay. In 2017 PEI finally began to provide abortion services, and the role of MASS shifted. These days the organization—now called Abortion Support Services Atlantic—primarily provides information. Its volunteers are people concerned about reproductive justice. Many are nursing or medical students. And many are people who have been helped by MASS in the past.

If you can't afford to get to a clinic, abortion isn't a real choice. We need to broaden our ideas of choice, and **if we give people a choice, it has to be real**.

—Shannon Hardy, founder of Maritime Abortion Support Services

CROWDFUNDING FOR ABORTION ACCESS

For many years, New Brunswick—one of Canada's Maritime provinces—had one private abortion clinic—the Morgentaler Clinic, in the city of Fredericton. Henry Morgentaler built the clinic and ran it for many years despite fierce opposition and constant harassment from protesters, who bought the building next door. But after Morgentaler's death, the clinic closed.

Adrian Edgar, a New Brunswick doctor, was concerned about how this would affect access to abortion for residents. Abortions were still available at two hospitals, in Moncton and Bathurst, but for those living in Fredericton this meant a two- or three-hour drive. And because New Brunswick hospitals have a waiting period between the mandatory counseling session and the procedure itself, patients would have to make the long trip twice.

So Adrian, his partner, Valerie Edelman, and a diverse group of people—the members of Reproductive Justice New Brunswick—got together to talk about how they could reopen the province's only abortion clinic. "We were sitting around in a circle, brainstorming: What can we do? And someone said, *Maybe we could do an online fundraiser*. Before we knew it, we had the call out, and we had donations coming in from all over the world."

Continued on p. 136

Continued from p. 135

The messages on the fundraising page show the support the campaign received. Some came from other clinics, with messages of solidarity. Some came from people who had had abortions themselves and wanted to help make sure that others had the same options. Some came from people who remembered the illegal-abortion era:

I am 80 years old. As a nurse in London in the 1950s, the first death I encountered was a 41-year-old mother who was poor and couldn't face having more children and suffered a botched abortion.

And some came from those who knew the long history of this battle:

Henry Morgentaler gave up a lucrative practice and went to jail in order for Canadian women to have reproductive rights. I'm not letting him down.

And many expressed outrage that a medical clinic in Canada—a country in which abortion is supposed to be accessible to all—was having to resort to crowdfunding.

The crowdfunding campaign was a success. The group raised enough money to lease the Morgentaler Clinic building and reopen it as Clinic 554. Adrian is one of the doctors who provides abortion services, and Valerie is the clinic manager. It isn't a perfect solution: The province of New Brunswick won't fund abortions done outside hospitals, making Clinic 554 the only clinic in the country that can't get government funding. And not everyone can afford to pay for an abortion. Still, there is now one more option for people facing unwanted pregnancies in New Brunswick.

Adrian Eoin Edgar and Valerie Edelman in front of Clinic 554.
The sign was made by the Fredericton Youth Feminists with help
from local artists Reid Lodge and Amber Chisholm.

USING SOCIAL MEDIA TO FIGHT ABORTION STIGMA

One of the ongoing challenges is the stigma that surrounds the topic of abortion. Although abortion is common, people often feel afraid to talk about it. When activists in France were fighting to liberalize abortion laws in the 1970s, one of the actions that helped bring about change was a **manifesto** signed by 343 famous women who spoke out about their own abortions.

Activists around the world are using similar strategies and speaking out about their abortions in order to fight stigma. And many are harnessing the power of the Internet to do so. Françoise Girard says, "When people are willing to come out and speak about their experiences, this is so powerful...For these young activists, social media gives them a level of connection and exchange across boundaries in a way we just didn't have thirty years ago."

In India, a feminist human rights organization called CREA has launched a campaign called #AbortTheStigma to encourage conversations about abortion, increase awareness, fight silence and shame, and challenge myths and misconceptions. Reproductive Choice Australia organized a flash mob on the streets of Adelaide to battle abortion stigma. And in Zambia, a youth-led organization called Africa First has embraced street theater, using singing, dancing and comedy to create conversations and reduce the stigma surrounding abortion and youth sexuality.

CREA produces resources to educate the public. The silence around abortion leads to misinformation and stigma, and makes it harder for people to access safe abortion.

137

Advocates for abortion access celebrate outside the Supreme Court after the Whole Woman's Health v. Hellerstedt ruling in 2016, a major victory for abortion rights. These activists' signs refer to the commonly cited statistic that one in three women would have an abortion by age 45. In 2017 a new study showed a decline in abortion rates, changing that figure to one in four.

In North America too, the battle for public opinion continues. While young people are more likely to support access to safe and legal abortion than the general population is, there's still much shame and stigma. This makes it difficult for people to talk about their abortions. The resulting silence around abortion reduces the support of the public, and anti-choice groups exploit this silence and shame.

The 1 in 3 Campaign takes on this challenge by encouraging conversation about abortion. Its website offers a place for people to share their stories—and the sharing of experiences is powerful. It is much more difficult to stigmatize abortion when you hear the stories of the individuals who have chosen to end their pregnancies.

"**Telling our stories** at full volume chips away at stigma, at lies, at the climate of shame that destroys the lives (sometimes literally) of women and girls and anyone anywhere on the gender spectrum who can become pregnant. **Abortion is common. Abortion is happening. Abortion needs to be legal, safe and accessible to everyone. Abortion is a thing you can say out loud.**"

—Lindy West, speaking about the #ShoutYourAbortion campaign to fight silence and stigma

YOUNG ACTIVISTS:
United States

Maddy Rasmussen is an eighteen-year-old high school student in Seattle, Washington, who has created a fantastic resource called the Safe Place Project, a website that lists every abortion clinic in the United States, with an interactive map and a list of restrictions to access for each state. Her website went live in the spring of 2017.

Maddy had been interested in women's rights for years, but her work as an intern at Legal Voice, an organization that advocates for marginalized women, deepened her awareness of many issues. "The issues around access to abortion and reproductive health shocked me the most," she says, "because it seemed like the biggest battle."

Her website began as a school project. "I'd started it in my junior year," she says. "Then when I needed to do my senior thesis project, I went back to it." She had some fears about the reaction her work might generate. "After the [2016] election, I was worried about having my name associated with the website. I was worried people would be like, *oh, she's doing the devil's work*. In the current political climate, with the defunding of Planned Parenthood, I was worried I could potentially become a target like abortion providers are. But I knew that if I was willing to do this, if I was able to put my name on it and own it, then women might be able to avoid barriers, and access care. So at the end of the day it was going to be worth it."

And so far, the feedback she has received has been overwhelmingly positive.

"Pay attention in your sex ed class,
and if there are things you need to know
or don't understand, talk to a teacher
or family member, or if you can't do that,
look it up on the Internet. It's better to learn
about it at a younger age."

—Maddy Rasmussen,
Safe Place Project, United States

MESSAGES TO READERS FROM ACTIVISTS INTERVIEWED IN BOOK

You are more powerful than you know. If you stand up and voice your opinions, you can create change in the world. I know that is an incredibly corny line, but it is something I believe with all my heart. It only takes one person to speak out to inspire the crowd. Never let someone silence you for any reason: what you have to say matters.

—Megan Brady, School Students for Choice, Ireland

Young people are taught to respect authority, and that adults have the answers—but adults are just people who have their own opinions and biases. It is okay to challenge authority, to ask questions, to challenge your teachers if they are giving you misinformation, to say, "Why aren't you teaching us about abortion, why aren't you teaching us about consent?"

—Renee Bracey Sherman, We Testify, National Network of Abortion Funds, United States

Young people have every right to a voice, every right to be curious and ask questions and to never ever accept the answer they hear from their parents or their family or their friends as the one true statement. The world is a complicated place, and every issue has many sides and many voices— don't be afraid to find your own. You can decide for yourself what you believe in. Never be afraid to fight for it.

—Niamh Scully, School Students for Choice, Ireland

Here's something young people can do: Speak up. Talk to your parents. Educate the people in your lives. Talk to older people about why abortion access matters to you.

—Adrian Eoin Edgar, Clinic 554, Canada

Don't take anything for granted...Know your rights and be ready to fight for them. Be proactive and daring. Truths surpass restrictions, borders and countries. Trust yourself, trust each other...We're stronger when we're organized in groups, parties, trade unions, etc. Be organized and be many.

—Hazal Atay, Youth Coalition for Sexual and Reproductive Rights, Women on Web, Turkey

I would like to tell young readers not to be afraid of being who they are. Despite rumors, gossip and different forms of persecution, to always stand for who they are and what they want.

—Lova Andrianina Randrianasolo, Youth Coalition for Sexual and Reproductive Rights, Youth First, Madagascar

Abortion is a perfectly safe and normal procedure, and getting pregnant is normal too. Your body is your own, and you have control over what you do with it, whether that means having sex or not, choosing to utilize contraception methods or forgoing sex completely.

—Stephanie Pineiro, Central Florida Women's Emergency Fund and We Testify Storyteller, United States

WHAT CAN YOU DO?

Abortion rights is a topic relevant to everyone! Regardless of your age and gender, you can educate yourself and others, you can fight against abortion stigma, and you can stand up for the rights of all people to make important choices about their own bodies.

- Demand comprehensive sex education. Know that you can ask questions and challenge your teachers if you are being given misinformation or if important topics are being left out of your sex ed classes. Learn the facts about reproductive health and about abortion.

- Know your rights. You have the right to have sex or not have sex, to access information about your body and your sexuality, to protect yourself from unwanted pregnancy, to end a pregnancy or continue it, and to be supported to make your own decisions. Make sure your friends know their rights too!

- Stand up against sexism, slut shaming, homophobia and transphobia. Sex is a normal part of most people's lives—it is not something shameful.

- Support pregnant and parenting teens. Make sure they are not excluded at your school, and speak up if they are treated badly.

- Support people who choose to have abortions. Be vocal about your support so friends know you are a safe person to turn to.

- Let people know that you support full reproductive rights and social justice for all people.

- Fundraise for groups that are working for change and supporting abortion access, in your own country or internationally!

- Amplify the voices of others who are working for change, and let your own voice be heard too. Social media can be so powerful!

THE REAL EXPERTS: LISTENING TO PEOPLE WHO HAVE HAD ABORTIONS

Reproductive rights will continue to face challenges—and those challenges will continue to be met by passionate, dedicated people who believe that people should be able to control their own bodies, choices and futures. No one knows what is needed better than those who are most directly affected—so reproductive rights activists are working hard to make sure that the voices of people who have had abortions are heard. One of those activists is Renee Bracey Sherman.

Renee is a reproductive justice and storytelling activist from Chicago, who now lives in Washington, DC. She shares her own abortion experience publicly to encourage others who have had abortions to speak out—and to push back against silence and stigma.

Renee was nineteen when she had an abortion. "I felt very alone, very isolated,"

Renee Bracey Sherman is committed to ensuring that the voices of people who've had abortions are at the center of conversations about reproductive rights.

she recalls. "Even though my parents are pro-choice, I was worried that they would judge me for having got pregnant in the first place."

After her own experience with abortion, she went on to become a powerful and passionate advocate for abortion rights—as a public speaker and writer, in her work as senior public affairs manager with the National Network of Abortion Funds, as a board member for NARAL Pro-Choice America and as an expert on abortion storytelling.

All too often we hear stories *about* people who have had abortions instead of stories by people who have *had* abortions.

"The abortion debate rages on, but the voices of those who've actually had abortions are ignored," Renee says. "Few people try to understand our lives. And we are never asked the most simple but important question: Why did you do it? That's intentional. It's easier to strip us of our rights when we're not treated as humans." Renee believes the voices of people who have had abortions should be at the center of conversations about reproductive rights, and she is helping to make this happen.

Renee is the founder and manager of We Testify, a program and website that support people in publicly sharing their abortion stories. "We are redefining who the experts are on abortion," she writes. "We Testify because we are the experts in our own lives, our abortion experiences and our truths. We know what's best for us and are in charge of our stories. We know that people are less likely to speak out if they don't see themselves represented."

As a biracial Black woman, Renee understands how deeply race is intertwined with abortion stigma. She says, "Stigma and oppression keep many of us from speaking out, and even when we do, we're faced with harassment and hatred…And sometimes, when stories are shared in the public sphere, they're by those with more privileges and power, continuing the lack of representation for the most marginalized and those experiencing the most barriers to care. But we believe we can change that."

Renee has written a guide to abortion storytelling called *Saying Abortion Aloud*. In 2015 Planned Parenthood honored her as one of 99 Dream Keepers to mark Black History Month, and Colorlines named her in its "16 Women of Color Who Made History in 2016" article.

Here is Renee's own abortion story.

Most mornings I hit the snooze alarm four or five times before I get up. I always have.

Story: Renee Bracey Sherman
Art: Kennedy Tarrell

5:45

BUTTERFLIES

But one morning, ten years ago, I didn't sleep in. I couldn't.

BLEGH

I did everything right.

These things don't happen to girls like me.

What exactly do you WEAR to your abortion?

I decided the standard jeans and a t-shirt were good enough. Comfortable. Simple.

HAHA

I learned I was pregnant the week before.

HAHAH

AHAHA

Haha, dude, she's SO TIRED. Your girlfriend's totally pregnant.

haha...

HAHA

ha...

It all made sense. The nausea. The fatigue. The swelling of my breasts.

I bolted.

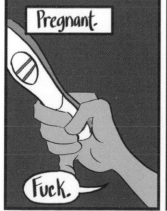

It's...

A normal waiting room.

$350. That's how much my abortion cost. I couldn't use my insurance because my parents would find out. I hadn't told them. I figured I would one day. Just not today.

Do you want sedation for an extra $100?

Have you eaten?

Do you have a ride home?

Do you want free birth control today?

Yes, no, yes, and sure?

I wished my mother was there with me.

We talked about abortion before. My mother and father were both nurses. They knew it was a safe medical procedure.

TAPTAPTAP   TAPTAP

Years later, I would tell her.

I'm sorry, I was afraid you wouldn't love me. I was afraid you'd think I was a failure.

I'm so proud of you.

Honey, you didn't let me down.

You made the best decision for you.

I am so proud to be your mother. Never forget that.

BUT FOR NOW, I WAS ALONE.

Renee?

The nurse was orthodox Jewish. I'd thought all religious people hated people who have abortions.

Her smile was warm and genuine. I trusted her.

Now when I say my abortion was amazing, I'm not kidding.

In TV and media, they talk about abortion providers as if they're evil. But that's just propaganda. Mine wasn't like that at all.

My doctor was caring. He made me smile.

Hellloooo, Renee!!!

And he looked curiously like Chef from South Park.

I hope that one day I get to meet him again and thank him.

Can you count back from 10 for me, Renee?

Her hands were soft. I imagine that's how my mom cared for her patients.

10...9...

She would have cared for me if she was here.

8...

7...6...

There were photos of butterflies taped to the ceiling. As I counted...

...I felt them fluttering.

They felt like... something new. Something reborn.

Like the moment I transformed my life.
Like love.

Renee, 19.

Renee, now.

Each one is a story. A metamorphosis.

STORY: RENEE BRACEY SHERMAN   ART: KENNEDY TARRELL

AUTHOR'S NOTE

I hope this book starts conversations. I think speaking about abortion is important: it is a part of many people's lives, and talking about it is a good way of fighting silence and stigma. But at the same time, no one should feel pressured to speak out about their own experience. Some cannot safely do so. Others may not be ready or may not want to. And that is okay too.

Before I became an author, I worked as a social worker. One of my jobs was in a women's health clinic in a Canadian hospital, where I spoke with many people who were getting abortions. Around this same time—the mid-to-late 1990s—doctors I worked with were receiving death threats. One abortion provider in our community was shot through the window of his own home. I saw how committed the doctors, nurses and clinic staff were to ensuring that people were able to access abortion services. And I saw, over and over, how vitally important it was for people to be able to end their pregnancies—to be in control of their own bodies and lives. I had always been pro-choice, but this experience deepened my understanding of the issue and strengthened my commitment to abortion rights.

The landscape with respect to abortion rights is changing rapidly. I have done my best to make sure that this book is up-to-date at the time of publication, but, of course, by the time you read it there will have been more changes. For that reason I've included websites in the Resources section that are good sources for current information.

I decided to write this book at the start of 2017, right after Donald Trump became president in the United States, because reproductive rights—and the rights of women, immigrants and refugees, people of color, people with disabilities and LGBTQ people—were under threat. This is a difficult time, but I feel confident that any future attacks on abortion rights will not go unchallenged. The worldwide community of people standing up for reproductive rights is dedicated, passionate and determined.

I think it is important for everyone to know the history of the abortion rights movement. Hard battles have been fought, and it is up to all of us to protect the ground that has been gained. We cannot afford to go back. When basic rights are threatened, it is vital that people speak up and resist. I hope this book will help young readers to do so.

GLOSSARY

abstinence-only education—programs that teach young people they should not have sex and do not teach other ways of avoiding pregnancy

agender—identifying as not having a gender

amniocentesis—a medical procedure for obtaining a sample of amniotic fluid in order to screen for developmental abnormalities in a fetus

anti-choice—opposed to people having a legal right to get an abortion

cervix—the narrow, cylinder-shaped neck of tissue that forms the lower part of the uterus and connects the uterus and the vagina

civil disobedience—refusal to obey laws as a form of peaceful protest, with the goal of bringing about change

colonialism—the practice by which a powerful country controls another country, occupying it with settlers and exploiting its resources to increase its own power and wealth

contraception—methods of preventing pregnancy from occurring; also referred to as birth control, family planning, pregnancy prevention or fertility control

crowdfunding—raising money for a project by asking for small donations from a large number of people, usually via the Internet

decriminalize—to cease to treat something as illegal or as a criminal offense

discrimination—actions or decisions that treat a person or group negatively because of their perceived race, sex, age, sexual orientation, gender identity, gender expression, religion or disability

emergency contraception—pill that can prevent pregnancy if taken within a specified period of time after sexual intercourse; also known as the morning-after pill or plan B

fanatical—holding extreme beliefs that may lead to unreasonable or violent behavior

first trimester—the first three months of a pregnancy

gender binary—the idea that there are only two genders

genderfluid—having a gender identity that shifts from day to day

gender identity—an internal sense of one's gender, which may or may not correspond with one's birth sex

gender-neutral pronouns—words such as *they* and *them* that identify a person as neither male nor female

genderqueer or *non-binary*—a person whose gender identity lies outside of traditional binary ideas of masculine and feminine

gestational limit—the point at which access to abortion services is restricted or denied, based on the duration of the pregnancy

harm-reduction model—an approach to public health that includes policies and practices designed to reduce the negative consequences associated with various human behaviors, while also supporting people's rights to make their own choices

ideology—a system of ideas and beliefs

induced abortion—the intentional or deliberate ending of a pregnancy

informed consent—permission granted by a patient to a doctor after being given full information about a procedure or treatment, including its possible risks and benefits

judicial bypass—an order given by a judge that allows a minor who meets certain criteria to have an abortion without notifying or getting consent from a parent

liberalization—the removal of bans or loosening of government restrictions on individual activities

lobbying—seeking to influence a politician or public official on an issue

manifesto—a written statement by a group in which it declares its beliefs, aims or intentions

marginalize—to treat a person, group or concept as insignificant or peripheral

medical abortion—a type of non-surgical abortion in which medication is used to end a pregnancy

midwife—a person trained to assist in childbirth

mifepristone—a medication typically used in combination with misoprostol to cause an abortion

miscarriage—the body's natural termination of a pregnancy before the fetus is developed enough to survive

misoprostol—a medication typically used in combination with mifepristone to cause an abortion

morning-after pill (also known as plan B)—a contraceptive pill that can prevent pregnancy if taken up to about seventy-two hours after having sex

Mifegymiso—a combination of two medications—mifepristone and misoprostol—used to cause an abortion; also known as RU-486 or the abortion pill

non-binary— see genderqueer

nongovernmental organizations (NGOs)—not-for-profit groups that operate independently of any government and work to address social or political issues

overturn—to change, invalidate or reverse a legal decision

propaganda—false, exaggerated or misleading information used to promote a particular political cause or point of view

referendum—a general vote by the electorate on a single political question

repeal—revoke or withdraw officially

reproductive justice—a framework that combines reproductive rights and social justice, focusing on the fundamental human right to have or not have children and to parent children in safe and sustainable communities

RU-486—a combination of two medications, mifepristone and misoprostol, that is used to induce an abortion; also known as the abortion pill

segregation—the separation of people based on their race, class or ethnicity; in the United States, this term can refer to the legally enforced separation of Black people under the "separate but equal" laws of the past and also to the socially enforced segregation which still exists

sepsis—a potentially life-threatening complication of an infection

sexual and reproductive health and rights (SRHR)—the concept of human rights applied to sexuality and reproduction

spontaneous abortion—the body's natural termination of a pregnancy before the fetus is developed enough to survive; also known as miscarriage

stigma—a strong feeling of disapproval, often based on negative and unfair beliefs that a society or group of people holds about a circumstance, quality or person

surgical abortion—a procedure that ends a pregnancy by dilating the cervix and using suction to remove the fetal tissue from the uterus

taboo—a social or religious custom prohibiting discussion of a particular subject or association with a particular person, place or thing

transgender—having a gender identity that differs from the sex a person was assigned at birth

trans-inclusive language—writing and speaking in ways that include trans and non-binary people

therapeutic abortions—abortions performed by a doctor; the term is used more specifically to describe abortions induced when a pregnancy poses a threat to the physical or mental health of the patient

women's liberation movement—the second wave of the feminist movement, beginning in the early 1960s and lasting until the early 1980s

RESOURCES

For more information about your body, your sexual and reproductive health, and how to protect yourself from unwanted pregnancy:
- Planned Parenthood: https://www.plannedparenthood.org/learn/teens.
- Scarleteen: Sex Ed for the Real World http://www.scarleteen.com/.
- All-Options: all-options.org or call toll-free 1-888-493-0092.

For comprehensive, current statistics and well-researched information about abortion, the Guttmacher Institute is a great resource: https://www.guttmacher.org/about.

For information about reproductive rights and health around the world, visit mariestopes.org.

Fact sheets about abortion—and information about its history and current challenges to access—are available from the National Abortion Federation: https://prochoice.org/education-and-advocacy/about-abortion/.

CBC Digital Archives contains many stories and video clips related to the history of abortion rights in Canada: http://www.cbc.ca/archives/categories/health/reproductive-issues/.

For the latest news and current events related to the issue of abortion rights, from a pro-reproductive rights perspective, check out Rewire: https://rewire.news/primary-topic/abortion/.

For articles about abortion written by women of color and non-binary people, Echoing Ida is a good resource: https://echoingida.org/issue_area/abortion/.

To learn more about the work done by Women on Waves, and to see photographs and video clips from their campaigns, visit their website: https://www.womenonwaves.org/.

You can also watch *Vessel*, a full-length documentary film about Women on Waves: http://vesselthefilm.com/.

Some of the comics in these pages came from the book *Comics for Choice*. It is an anthology of comics about abortion, featuring many diverse voices and ranging from abortion history and politics to personal stories and activism. You can order a copy or download it for free or by donation at http://comicsforchoice.com/.

REFERENCES

INTRODUCTION

Abortion Rights Coalition of Canada. "Statistics—Abortion in Canada." Abortion Rights Coalition of Canada, April 2017. arcc-cdac.ca/backrounders/statistics-abortion-in-canada.pdf.

Guttmacher Institute. "Induced Abortion in the United States." Guttmacher Institute, October 2017. guttmacher.org/fact-sheet/induced-abortion-united-states.

University of Ottawa. "Society, the Individual and Medicine: Facts and Figures on Abortion in Canada." University of Ottawa, July 2015. med.uottawa.ca/sim/data/abortion_e.htm.

CHAPTER ONE

Abbott, Karen. "Madame Restell: The Abortionist of Fifth Avenue." Smithsonian.com, Nov. 27, 2012. smithsonianmag.com/history/madame-restell-the-abortionist-of-fifth-avenue-145109198/.

Boston Women's Health Collective. "Women and Their Bodies: A Course." Our Bodies, Ourselves, 1970. ourbodiesourselves.org/cms/assets/uploads/2014/04/Women-and-Their-Bodies-1970.pdf.

Bracey Sherman, Renee. "What the War on Reproductive Rights Has to do With Poverty and Race." *Yes! Magazine*, May 25, 2016. yesmagazine.org/peace-justice/what-the-war-on-reproductive-rights-has-to-do-with-poverty-and-race-20160525.

Dore, Mary, dir. *She's Beautiful When She's Angry*. New York: International Film Circuit and She's Beautiful Film Project, 2014. 92 minutes.

Gold, Rachel Benson. "Lessons from Before Roe: Will Past be Prologue?" *Guttmacher Policy Review* 6, no. 1. March 1, 2003. guttmacher.org/gpr/2003/03/lessons-roe-will-past-be-prologue.

Morrison, Patt. "Lest We Forget the Era Preceding Roe vs. Wade." *Los Angeles Times*, Jan. 21, 2003. http://articles.latimes.com/2003/jan/21/local/me-patt21.

Our Bodies, Ourselves. "History." About. ourbodiesourselves.org/history/.

Ross, Loretta, and Rickie Solinger. *Reproductive Justice: An Introduction*. Oakland: University of California Press, 2017.

Soranus of Ephesus. *Soranus' Gynecology*. Translated by Owsei Temkin. Baltimore: John Hopkins University Press, 1956.

Stortz, Gerald J., with Murray A. Eaton. "Pro Bono Publico: The Eastview Birth Control Trial." *Atlantis* 8, no. 2 (Spring/Printemps 1983): 51–60. http://journals.msvu.ca/index.php/atlantis/article/viewFile/4530/3768.

Wolfe, Jessica Duffin. "Why I Am an Abortion Doctor, by Garson Romalis" (speech at University of Toronto Law School Symposium, Jan. 25, 2008). *Toronto Review of Books*, Oct. 29, 2012. torontoreviewofbooks.com/2012/10/why-i-am-an-abortion-doctor-by-dr-garson-romalis/.

CHAPTER TWO

Arthur, Joyce. "Abortion in Canada: History, Law, and Access." 1999. hackcanada.com/canadian/freedom/canadabort.html.

Brownmiller, Susan. "Everywoman's Abortions: 'The Oppressor Is Man.'" *Village Voice*, March 27, 1969. https://womenwhatistobedone.files.wordpress.com/2013/09/1968-03-27-village-voice-full.pdf.

Connolley, Greg. "Pro-Abortion Protest: House Screams to a Halt." *Ottawa Citizen*, May 12, 1970.

Day, Shelagh, and Stan Persky, eds. *The Supreme Court of Canada Decision on Abortion*. Vancouver: New Star, 1988.

Dunlap, Bridgette. "How Clergy Set the Standard for Abortion Care." *The Atlantic*, May 29, 2016. theatlantic.com/politics/archive/2016/05/how-the-clergy-innovated-abortion-services/484517.

Joffe, Carole. *Doctors of Conscience: The Struggle to Provide Abortion before and after Roe V. Wade*. Boston: Beacon Press, 1996. Quotes from pp. 12 and 82.

Kaplan, Laura. *The Story of Jane: The Legendary Underground Feminist Abortion Service*. Chicago: University of Chicago Press, 1995. Quotes from introduction and p. 287.

Kieran, Sheila. "The Struggle for Abortion Rights: 1960s to 1980s." *The Morgentaler Decision*, n.d. morgentaler25years.ca/the-struggle-for-abortion-rights/1960s-to-1980s/.

Mackie, Victor. "Protesters Force House to Adjourn—Women Carry 'Abortion War' into Commons Gallery." *Winnipeg Free Press*, May 12, 1970.

McCook, Sheila. "Pleas for Abortion Greeted by Silence." *Ottawa Citizen*, May 11, 1970.

McKenna, Brian. "MPs Study Ways to Curb Disruptions." *Montreal Star*, May 12, 1970.

Our Bodies, Ourselves. "History of Abortion in the U.S." March 28, 2014. ourbodiesourselves.org/health-info/u-s-abortion-history/.

Rebick, Judy. *Ten Thousand Roses: The Making of a Feminist Revolution*. Toronto: Penguin Canada, 2005. Quote from p. xv.

Religious Coalition for Reproductive Choice. "History." http://rcrc.org/history/.

Sanger, Clyde. "Angry Women Halt Sitting of Parliament." *Globe and Mail*, May 12, 1970.

Tierney, Ben. "Our View: Freedom to Decide." *Calgary Herald*, May 12, 1970.

CHAPTER THREE

Abortion Rights Coalition of Canada. "Position Paper #58: The Injustice and Harms of Parental Consent Laws for Abortion." October 2017. arcc-cdac.ca/postionpapers/58-Parental-Consent.pdf.

American Civil Liberties Union. "Laws Restricting Teenagers Access to Abortion." aclu.org/other/laws-restricting-teenagers-access-abortion?redirect=reproductive-freedom/laws-restricting-teenagers-access-abortion.

Arthur, Joyce, Rebecca Bailin, Kathy Dawson, Megan Glenwright, Autumn Reinhardt-Simpson, Meg Sykes and Alison Zimmer. "Review of 'Crisis Pregnancy Centre' Websites in Canada." Abortion Rights Coalition of Canada, May 2016. arcc-cdac.ca/CPC-study/CPC-Website-Study-ARCC-2016.pdf.

Boonstra, Heather D. "Abortion in the Lives of Women Struggling Financially: Why Insurance Coverage Matters." *Guttmacher Policy Review* 19 (July 14, 2016). guttmacher.org/gpr/2016/07/abortion-lives-women-struggling-financially-why-insurance-coverage-matters.

Bracey Sherman, Renee. "What the War on Reproductive Rights Has to do With Poverty and Race." *Yes! Magazine*, May 25, 2016. yesmagazine.org/peace-justice/what-the-war-on-reproductive-rights-has-to-do-with-poverty-and-race-20160525.

Bracey Sherman, Renee. "Who Should You Listen to on Abortion? People Who've Had Them." *New York Times*, May 20, 2017. nytimes.com/2017/05/20/opinion/sunday/abortion-people-whove-had-them.html.

Catholics for Choice. "About Us." catholicsforchoice.org/about-us/.

Center for Reproductive Rights. "Evaluating Priorities: Measuring Women's and Children's Health and Well-being against Abortion Restrictions in the States—Volume II." August 1, 2017. reproductiverights.org/EvaluatingPriorities.

Deibel, Kersha. "Kersha's Story." We Testify: Our Abortion Stories. https://wetestify.org/stories/kershas-story/.

DePass, Tanya. "Tanya Depass's Abortion Story." We Testify: Our Abortion Stories. https://wetestify.org/stories/tanya-depass-abortion-story/.

Essert, Matt. "The States with the Highest Teenage Birth Rates Have One Thing in Common." Mic, Sept. 14, 2015. https://mic.com/articles/98886/the-states-with-the-highest-teenage-birth-rates-have-one-thing-in-common#.eGIOKThhH.

Groen, Danielle. "When It Comes to Abortion, Do Medical Schools Need to Smarten Up?" *Chatelaine*, Feb. 17, 2015. chatelaine.com/living/features-living/abortion-education-canada-medical-schools-smarten-up/.

Guttmacher Institute. "Targeted Regulation of Abortion Providers." Dec. 1, 2017. guttmacher.org/state-policy/explore/targeted-regulation-abortion-providers.

Jane's Due Process. "Who Gets a Judicial Bypass?" June 14, 2017. https://janesdueprocess.org/blog/gets-judicial-bypass/.

Jerman, Jenna, Rachel K. Jones and Tsuyoshi Onda. "Characteristics of Abortion Patients in 2014 and Changes Since 2008." Guttmacher Institute, May 2016. guttmacher.org/report/characteristics-us-abortion-patients-2014.

Joffe, Carole. *Dispatches from the Abortion Wars: The Costs of Fanaticism to Doctors, Patients, and the Rest of Us.* Boston: Beacon Press, 2011.

Joyce, Kathryn. "Meet the Medical Students for Choice." *Conscience Magazine*, June 29, 2015. consciencemag.org/2015/06/29/meet-the-medical-students-for-choice/.

Kost, Kathryn, Isaac Maddow-Zimet and Alex Arpaia. "Pregnancies, Births and Abortions Among Adolescents and Young Women in the United States." Guttmacher Institute, September 2017. guttmacher.org/report/us-adolescent-pregnancy-trends-2013.

Martin, Nina. "The Supreme Court Decision That Made a Mess of Abortion Rights." *Mother Jones*, Feb. 29, 2016. motherjones.com/politics/2016/02/supreme-court-decision-mess-abortion-rights/.

Mickleburgh, Rod. "Garson Romalis Risked His Life to Perform Abortions." *Globe and Mail*, Feb. 21, 2014. theglobeandmail.com/news/british-columbia/garson-romalis-risked-his-life-to-perform-abortions/article17052093/?page=all.

National Abortion Federation. "Abortion Myths." https://prochoice.org/education-and-advocacy/about-abortion/abortion-myths/.

National Women's Law Center. "The Hyde Amendment Creates an Unacceptable Barrier to Women Getting Abortions." April 21, 2017. https://nwlc.org/resources/hyde-amendment-creates-unacceptable-barrier-women-getting-abortions/.

O'Brien, Jon. "The Catholic Case for Abortion Rights." *Time* online. September 22, 2015. Accessed at time.com/4045227/the-catholic-case-for-abortion-rights/.

Parker, Willie. *Life's Work: A Moral Argument for Choice.* New York: Simon & Schuster, 2017. Quotes from pp. 6 and 9.

Rankin, Lauren. "What It's Really Like to Be a Volunteer Escort at an Abortion Clinic." *HuffPost*, Dec. 2, 2015. huffingtonpost.com/lauren-rankin/what-its-like-volunteer-escort-abortion-clinic_b_8700370.html.

Stanger-Hall, Kathrin F., and David W. Hall. "Abstinence-Only Education and Teen Pregnancy Rates: Why We Need Comprehensive Sex Education in the U.S." *PLoS ONE* 6, no. 10 (2011). ncbi.nlm.nih.gov/pmc/articles/PMC3194801/.

United States House of Representatives, Committee on Government Reform—Minority Staff, Special Investigations Division."The Content of Federally Funded Abstinence-Only Education Programs." Prepared for Rep. Henry A. Waxman, December 2004. spot.colorado.edu/~tooley/HenryWaxman.pdf.

Wiebe, Ellen R., Lisa Littman, Janusz Kaczorowski and Erin Moshier. "Misperceptions About the Risks of Abortion in Women Presenting for Abortion." *Journal of Obstetrics and Gynaecology Canada* 36, no. 3 (March 2014): 223–230. jogc.com/article/S1701-2163(15)30630-7/pdf.

Williams, Amanda. "Why I Testified in Texas." We Testify: Our Abortion Stories. https://wetestify.org/stories/why-i-testified-in-texas/.

Willow Women's Clinic. "Myths and Facts About Abortion." 2010. willowclinic.ca/?page_id=287.

Wolfe, Jessica Duffin. "Why I Am an Abortion Doctor, by Garson Romalis" (speech at University of Toronto Law School Symposium, Jan. 25, 2008). *Toronto Review of Books*, Oct. 29, 2012. torontoreviewofbooks.com/2012/10/why-i-am-an-abortion-doctor-by-dr-garson-romalis/.

CHAPTER FOUR

BBC News. "Black Monday: Polish Women Strike Against Abortion Ban." Oct. 3, 2016. bbc.com/news/world-europe-37540139.

Burns-Pieper, Annie. "Trump Changes to Foreign Aid Restricting Access to Family Planning Services in Poorest Countries." CBC News, Sept. 16, 2017. cbc.ca/news/world/mexico-city-policy-affecting-madagascar-and-zimbabwe-1.4284893.

Casey, Ruairi. "Ireland's Overwhelming Vote to Repeal Abortion Restrictions Is New Evidence of a Changed Nation." *Los Angeles Times*, May 26, 2018. latimes.com/world/la-fg-ireland-abortion-referendum-20180526-story.html.

Davies, Christian. "Poland's Abortion Ban Proposal Near Collapse after Mass Protests." *Guardian*, Oct. 5, 2016. theguardian.com/world/2016/oct/05/polish-government-performs-u-turn-on-total-abortion-ban.

Gambino, Lauren. "Women's Rights Groups Brace for Trump: 'We Are Used to Fighting Impossible Odds.' *Guardian*, Nov. 18, 2016. theguardian.com/society/2016/nov/18/womens-right-groups-fight-trump-pence-abortion-birth-control.

Gemzell-Danielsson, Kristina, and Amanda Cleeve. "Estimating Abortion Safety: Advancements and Challenges." *Lancet* 390, no. 10110 (2017): 2333–2334. thelancet.com/journals/lancet/article/PIIS0140-6736(17)32135-9/fulltext.

Gorlick, Adam. "Abortions in Africa Increase Despite Republican Policy to Curb Payment for Procedures." *Stanford Report*, September 28, 2011. http://news.stanford.edu/news/2011/september/abortion-africa-policy-092811.html.

Gunter, Joel. "Abortion in Ireland: The Fight for Choice." BBC News, March 8, 2017. bbc.com/news/world-europe-39183423.

Guttmacher Institute. "Adding It Up: Investing in Contraception and Maternal and Newborn Health, 2017." guttmacher.org/fact-sheet/adding-it-up-contraception-mnh-2017.

Guttmacher Institute. "Induced Abortion Worldwide." September 2017. guttmacher.org/fact-sheet/induced-abortion-worldwide.

Haddad, Lisa B., and Nawal M. Nour. "Unsafe Abortion: Unnecessary Maternal Mortality." *Reviews in Obstetrics and Gynecology* 2.2 (2009): 122–126. ncbi.nlm.nih.gov/pmc/articles/PMC2709326/.

Human Rights Watch. "Trump's 'Mexico City Policy' or 'Global Gag Rule': Questions and Answers." Human Rights Watch, updated June 22, 2017. hrw.org/news/2017/06/22/trump-mexico-city-policy-or-global-gag-rule.

Hunter, Molly, and Fergal Gallagher. "Irish From All Over the World Are Flying Home to Vote in Ireland's Abortion Referendum."ABC News, May 24, 2018. abcnews.go.com/International/irish-world-flying-home-vote-irelands-abortion-referendum/story?id=55380085.

Independent.ie Video Team. "'Ireland Has Lit a Beacon of Hope for Countries All Over the World'—Together for Yes campaign." Video produced for *The Independent*, 2:21, May 27, 2018. independent.ie/videos/irish-news/watch-ireland-has-lit-a-beacon-of-hope-for-countries-all-over-the-world-together-for-yes-campaign-36950876.html.

International Women's Health Coalition. "Trump's Global 'Protecting Life' Policy Endangers Lives." May 16, 2017. https://iwhc.org/2017/05/trumps-global-protecting-life-policy-endangers-lives/.

Irish Family Planning Association. "Abortion in Ireland: Statistics." 2016. ifpa.ie/Hot-Topics/Abortion/Statistics.

Mundasad, Smitha. "Abortion Study: 25% of Pregnancies Terminated, Estimates Suggest." BBC News, May 12, 2016. bbc.com/news/health-36266873.

Sang-Hun, Choe. "South Korea Confronts Open Secret of Abortion." *New York Times*, Jan. 5, 2010. nytimes.com/2010/01/06/world/asia/06korea.html.

Sherwood, Harriet. "Savita Halappanavar's Father Thanks Irish Voters for 'Historic' Abortion Vote." *Guardian* (international edition), May 26, 2018. theguardian.com/world/2018/may/26/savita-halappanavar-father-thanks-irish-voters-for-historic-abortion-vote.

Smyth, Catherine. "Abortion: UK 'Breaches NI's Women's Rights.'" BBC News, Feb. 23, 2018. http://bbc.com/news/uk-northern-ireland-43167255.

Whitten, Diana, dir. *Vessel*. United States: Sovereignty Productions, in association with Fork Films, Impact Partners, and Chicken and Egg Pictures. 2014. 1 hr. 26 min.

World Health Organization. "Unsafe Abortion Incidence and Mortality." World Health Organization, 2012. http://apps.who.int/iris/bitstream/10665/75173/1/WHO_RHR_12.01_eng.pdf.

CHAPTER FIVE

Abortion Rights Coalition of Canada. "Position Paper #100: Why ARCC Supports Reproductive Justice." December 2015. arcc-cdac.ca/postionpapers/100-reproductive-justice.pdf.

American Civil Liberties Union. "After a Month of Obstruction by the Trump Administration, Jane Doe Gets Her Abortion." American Civil Liberties Union and the ACLU Foundation, Oct. 25, 2017. aclu.org/news/after-month-obstruction-trump-administration-jane-doe-gets-her-abortion.

Barar, Rana. "Rana Barar's Abortion Story." We Testify: Our Abortion Stories. https://wetestify.org/stories/rana-barars-abortion-story/.

Bracey Sherman, Renee. "Who Should You Listen to on Abortion? People Who've Had Them." *New York Times*, May 20, 2017. nytimes.com/2017/05/20/opinion/sunday/abortion-people-whove-had-them.html.

Bracey Sherman, Renee. "We Testify's Origin Story." We Testify: Our Abortion Stories. August 2016. https://wetestify.org/stories/we-testifys-origin-story/.

CBC News. "Abortion Pills Accessed Online Are as Safe, Effective as Clinics: Study." May 16, 2017. cbc.ca/news/health/medical-abortion-telemedicine-1.4118688.

CREA. "#Abort the Stigma: For Safe Abortion Access and Reproductive Justice." creaworld.org/abortthestigma.

Cruz, Caitlin. "Dr. Willie Parker Wants to Take Back the Moral High Ground on Abortion." *Rolling Stone*, April 10, 2017. rollingstone.com/politics/features/willie-parker-taking-back-the-moral-high-ground-on-abortion-w475403.

Grant, Kelly. "Abortion Pill's Canadian Launch Delayed by Lack of Coverage, Distribution Rules." *Globe and Mail*, updated March 23, 2017. theglobeandmail.com/news/national/abortion-pills-canadian-launch-delayed-by-lack-of-coverage-distribution-rules/article34181063/.

Gutiérrez, Jack Qu'emi. "Jack Qu'emi Gutiérrez's Abortion Story." We Testify. https://wetestify.org/stories/jack-quemi-gutierrezs-abortion-story/.

Hernandez, Yamani. "Want to Win on Abortion? Talk About It as an Issue of Love, Compassion." *Rewire*, June 7, 2017. https://rewire.news/article/2017/06/07/want-win-abortion-talk-issue-love-compassion/.

Ipas. "Using Street Theater to Teach About Safe Abortion." Ipas, Aug. 3, 2016. http://spotlight.ipas.org/using-street-theater-to-teach-about-safe-abortion.

Landers, Elizabeth. "Vice President Mike Pence Speech Right at Home at March for Life." CNN, updated Jan. 27, 2017. cnn.com/2017/01/27/politics/mike-pence-march-for-life-speech/index.html.

1 in 3 Campaign. "1 in 3." 1 in 3 Campaign: A Project of Advocates for Youth. http://1in3campaign.org/.

Parker, Willie. *Life's Work: A Moral Argument for Choice.* New York: Simon and Schuster, 2017. Quotes from p. 27.

Planned Parenthood Toronto. "Trans and Nonbinary Youth Inclusivity in Sexual Health Guidelines for Sexual Health Service Providers and Educators." April 2016. ppt.on.ca/ppt/wp-content/uploads/2016/04/Trans-and-nonbinary-youth-inclusivity-in-sexual-health-guidelines-FINAL.pdf.

Reproductive Justice New Brunswick. "Help Us Ensure Access to Safe Abortion in N.B." FundRazr, 2014. https://fundrazr.com/campaigns/aoCmf.

Richards, Cecile. "Planned Parenthood Action Fund's Statement on Donald Trump's Election as Next President of the United States." Planned Parenthood press release, Nov. 9, 2016. plannedparenthoodaction.org/pressroom/planned-parenthood-action-funds-statement-donald-trumps-election-next-president-of-the-united-states.

Ross, Loretta. "Understanding Reproductive Justice." Trust Black Women, updated March 2011. trustblackwomen.org/our-work/what-is-reproductive-justice/9-what-is-reproductive-justice.

West, Lindy. "I Set Up #ShoutYourAbortion Because I Am Not Sorry, and I Will Not Whisper." *Guardian*, Sept. 22, 2015. theguardian.com/commentisfree/2015/sep/22/i-set-up-shoutyourabortion-because-i-am-not-sorry-and-i-will-not-whisper.

PHOTO CREDITS

p. 3: Courtesy of the Global Justice Center

Introduction: p. 8: Warren K. Leffler, U.S. News & World Report Collection, Library of Congress; p. 9: Sebastian Kaczorowski/iStockphoto.com; p. 11: courtesy of Women on Waves Foundation; pp. 12–13: courtesy of the National Network of Abortion Funds

Chapter One: p. 15: Wikimedia Commons; p. 17: Heather Ault/4000 Years for Choice; p. 19: courtesy of the Atwater Collection of American Popular Medicine, Edward G. Miner Library, University of Rochester; p. 20 (clockwise from top): Wikimedia Commons, Wikimedia Commons, Library of Congress (*New York Herald*, April 13, 1840), Wikimedia Commons; p. 21: courtesy of *Journal of Obstetrics and Gynaecology Canada* (JOGC); p. 24: Ben Holbrook, courtesy of Judy Rebick; p. 25: Joseph A. Labadie Collection, University of Michigan (CC BY 4.0); p. 27: Bev Grant/Getty, second-wave feminist, photojournalist and member of New York Radical Women; p. 28: courtesy of Elliott Landy

Chapter Two: pp. 32–33: courtesy of Judson Memorial Church; p. 34: Bev Grant/Getty, second-wave feminist, photojournalist and member of New York Radical Women; p. 35: public domain; p. 36: *Comics for Choice*, excerpt from "Jane," written by Rachel Wilson, art by Ally Shwed; p. 39: courtesy of Women Make Movies; p. 40: courtesy of Steve Woit; p. 41: Leif Skoogfors/Camera Press/Redux; p. 42: Lorie Shaull/Wikimedia Commons; p. 43: courtesy of York University Libraries, Clara Thomas Archives & Special Collections, Toronto Telegram fonds, ASCASC06160; p. 44: courtesy of Sarah N. Harvey; p. 46: The Canadian Press/Chuck Mitchell; p. 48: courtesy of Errol Young; p. 50: courtesy of Jackie Larkin; p. 53: Edward Regan/*The Globe and Mail*; p. 55: Jarrah Hodge, courtesy of Joyce Arthur

Chapter Three: p. 58: Chad Griffith, courtesy of Dr. Willie Parker/Religious Coalition for Reproductive Choice; p. 61: Drew Altizer Photography; p. 62: courtesy of Medical Students for Choice; p. 63: courtesy of David Imbago Jácome; p. 64: courtesy of Benita Ulisano; p. 65: Rena Schild/Shutterstock.com; p. 68: courtesy of If/When/How: Lawyering for Reproductive Justice; p. 69: from Jane's Due Process 2016 Impact Report; p. 70: courtesy of Stephanie Pineiro; p. 74: NARAL Pro-Choice America/Flickr (CC BY 2.0); p. 78: courtesy of Catholics for Choice; p. 80: Joel Carillet/iStockphoto.com.

Chapter Four: p. 85: worldabortionlaws.com/map; p. 86: Michael Stravato; p. 88: *Comics for Choice*, excerpt from "Undue Burdens," by Hallie Jay Pope; p. 91: courtesy of the Global Justice Center; p. 92: courtesy of EVA (Education As Vaccine); p. 93: Creative Commons/Wikimedia (CC BY-SA 4.0); pp. 94–95: William Murphy, Flickr (CC BY-SA 2.0); p. 96: courtesy of School Students for Choice; p. 97: Alastair Moore; p. 98: EPA/Aidan Crawley; pp. 99–101: courtesy of School Students for Choice; p. 103: praszkiewicz/Shutterstock.com; p. 104: Irontrybex/Dreamstime.com; p. 105: Ringel Goslinga; p. 106: courtesy of Women on Waves Foundation; p. 107: Marc Godefroy, courtesy of Women on Waves Foundation; p. 108: Willow Paule, courtesy of Women on Waves Foundation; p. 110: courtesy of Women on Web; pp. 111–112: courtesy of Hazal Atay; p. 113: courtesy of the National Network of Abortion Funds; pp. 114–115: courtesy of Lova Andrianina Randrianasolo; pp. 116–117: courtesy of Isabel Pérez Witzke.

Chapter Five: p. 120: courtesy of the Wilson Center; p. 121: courtesy of Sister Song; p. 123: Lorie Shaull/Flickr (CC BY-SA 2.0); p. 124: courtesy of Physicians for Reproductive Health; p. 126: John Lehmann/*The Globe and Mail*; p. 128: courtesy of the National Network of Abortion Funds; p. 131: Lauryn Gutierrez © *Rewire.News*; p. 133: *Comics for Choice*, excerpt from "Choices," written by Yamani Hernandez, art by Sharon Rimann; p. 134: courtesy of Ian Selig; p. 136: courtesy of Adrian Eoin Edgar; p. 137: creaworld.org/abortthestigma; p. 138: courtesy of Advocates for Youth; p. 139: #ShoutYourAbortion and PM Press; pp. 140–141: courtesy of Maddy Rasmussen; p. 145: courtesy of the National Network of Abortion Funds; pp. 147–155: *Comics for Choice*, "Butterflies," written by Renee Bracey Sherman with art by Kennedy Tarrell

Every effort has been made to locate and credit the correct copyright owners of the images used in this book. The publisher apologizes for any errors or omissions and would be grateful if notified of corrections that should be made in future reprints or editions.

ACKNOWLEDGMENTS

One of the best parts of writing this book was that it gave me the opportunity to speak with—and learn from—so many brilliant people. Many, many thanks to everyone who helped: answering my questions, sharing knowledge and experiences, and inspiring me with their passion and dedication. People were so encouraging and excited about the book, and very generous, thoughtful and insightful. I only wished I could find the room in this book to include more quotes, more information, more stories. I am enormously grateful to everyone who helped me with this project—there are too many of you to name, but the following people made particularly important contributions. Any flaws, omissions and mistakes are, of course, my own!

To my very dear friend Pat Smith, thank you so much for encouraging me to write this book, for introducing me to activists and physicians, and for giving me feedback on my ideas and my words throughout the writing process. This book wouldn't exist without you.

Special thanks also to Renee Bracey Sherman, who shared her extensive knowledge, insight and experience as a reproductive justice advocate and expert on abortion storytelling: I found our conversations extremely helpful. Renee also introduced me to others whose words, stories and artwork became an important part of this book—and she allowed me to include her own abortion story, which became the final (and beautiful) pages of this book. It made the perfect ending, and I am so very grateful.

Canadian activists Joyce Arthur, Jackie Larkin and Judy Rebick were all tremendously helpful, bringing to life the history of the abortion rights movement in Canada and deepening my understanding of current issues as well. Sociologist and reproductive rights advocate Carole Joffe did the same for abortion rights history and issues south of the border, both through her comprehensive books and by answering all my emailed questions. Amanda Bennett of Jane's Due Process helped me understand the judicial bypass process and the experiences of the teens who go through it. Canadian physician and reproductive rights advocate Ellen Wiebe took the time to help me learn about medical abortion and telemedicine, and New Brunswick doctor Adrian Eoin Edgar explained the difficulties of abortion access in Canada's

Maritime provinces and spoke with me about trans-inclusion issues as well. Trystan Angel Reese also helped me better understand reproductive rights issues for transgender people. Thank you all.

Françoise Girard of the International Women's Health Coalition shared her expertise on reproductive rights and health in a global context—and her passion for the subject was infectious. Both Françoise and Sarah Hedges-Chou of the Youth Coalition for Sexual and Reproductive Rights connected me with activists around the world. Thank you both so much—your support made this book so much better.

And to all the activists whose words, stories and photographs appear in these pages: I can't express how much I enjoyed speaking with you all. Fadekemi Akinfaderin-Agarau, Hazal Atay, Megan Brady, Jodie Doyle, Shannon Hardy, David Imbago Jácome, Stephanie Pineiro, Lova Andrianina Randrianasolo, Maddy Rasmussen, Niamh Scully and Isabel Pérez Witzke: You all inspire me. Thank you so much for helping me and for all that you do to make our world a better place.

I am also very grateful to all the people who read the manuscript and gave me such thoughtful feedback: Heidi Darroch, Eli Darroch, Maya Hope-Cleves, Cheryl May, Pat Smith, Ilse Stevenson and Giles Stevenson. Thank you all so much.

Thank you to all the artists and photographers who shared their work. Hazel Newlevant, who edited the wonderful book *Comics for Choice*, helped me connect with the artists and writers whose work appears in these pages.

To Andrew Wooldridge of Orca Book Publishers: thank you so much for saying yes, again. To my talented editor, Sarah Harvey: I loved working with you on this, and it meant so much to me to know that you share my passion for this subject. Art director and designer Teresa Bubela not only put countless hours into making this book look beautiful, but also understood what was important to me and worked hard to reflect those priorities in the images and design. Thanks also to Meags Fitzgerald for her wonderful illustrations. And to everyone in the Orca pod: as always, thank you. You are the best team to work with, and I couldn't be luckier.

And finally, an extra thank-you hug to my wonderful parents, my partner and my son, who love and support me in so many ways and who have spent countless hours listening to me talk about reproductive rights.

INDEX

Page numbers in **bold** indicate an image caption.

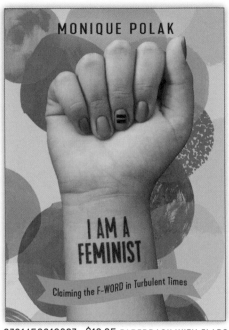

9781459818927 • $19.95 PAPERBACK WITH FLAPS

What is feminism? Why does it still matter? What exactly does intersectionality mean? In order to answer these (and many other questions) *I Am a Feminist* first examines the history of feminism and then addresses the issues girls and women continue to face today. The book also looks at the ways in which people, especially young people, are working together to create a world where gender equality is a reality, not a dream.